FULL CIRCLE

The Story of Worthing's Connaught Theatre

FULL CIRCLE

The Story of Worthing's Connaught Theatre

JOHN WILLMER

Optimus Books, Worthing

First published in Great Britain by Optimus Books Ltd 1999

ISBN 0953313220

A full CIP record for this book is available from the British Library

We acknowledge, with many thanks, permission to quote from the following publications: Peter Cushing, *An Autobiography* (published by Arthur Barker); Leslie Sands, *Tuppence for the Rainbow*; *Radio Times; The Stage* Newspaper Ltd; *Brighton and Hove Herald* and *Sussex Daily News* (Newsquest (Sussex) Ltd), the *Worthing Gazette* and *Worthing Herald* (T.R.Beckett Ltd); *Sightline,* the Journal of the Association of British Theatre Technicians and Disley Jones; *The Kenneth Williams Diaries*, edited by Russell Davies and published by HarperCollins Publishers Ltd. and *Plays and Players* Applause for extracts from *Theatre World.*

Thanks for permission to reproduce photographs are due to Walter Gardiner Photography, Freddie Feest and T.R.Beckett Ltd. Every effort has been made to trace all copyright-holders but if any have been inadvertently overlooked the publishers and author will be pleased to remedy any omission at the first opportunity.

Optimus Books Ltd
27 Warwick Street
Worthing
West Sussex
BN11 3DQ

Layout & Design by Bill & Darren Holdstock Graphic Designs Worthing
Printed and bound in Great Britain by Biddles Ltd, Guildford

FOREWORD

Sir Alan Ayckbourn, C.B.E.

It was the stuff of every young, aspiring actor's dreams.

In the late fifties, at the age of 17 or 18, I was at Worthing as an (unpaid) ASM working in all departments but with my hopes always set on small-part stage appearances which occasionally cropped up. I knew that, given the right break, my innate star quality would immediately be recognised. Worthing in those days was a weekly rep. The schedule was a punishing one - young actors today, if you describe it to them, look at you in blank astonishment or shake their heads sadly at the tricks old people's memories can play.

I was working in the scenic workshop when it happened. The current show had opened on the Monday, the next production was already under way when one of the cast had 'done a runner'. The pressure had finally got to him and he had vanished overnight. I was summoned to the manager's office and offered the part. Could I learn it and be ready to go on that night? "Of course", I replied, youthfully unhesitating. "Yes sir!" Six long months in show business and a break at last!

In the event I got through that Tuesday performance in a shallow trance. My voice, whenever I chanced to remember to speak, appeared to be coming from a deep well. Most of my lines, I seem to recall, were spoken by the leading man, Peter Byrne, who adroitly managed to hold long seamless conversations with himself. I was aware, throughout the show, of continuous, off-putting heavy breathing which I later identified as my own.

At the end of the performance the manager came to me smiling, shook me by the hand, thanked me and told me the good news that a real actor would be arriving for the Wednesday matinee the following day.

I returned to the scene dock, chastened by the harshness of theatrical reality. It was seven years before the message finally sunk in and I finally gave up acting forever.

Nonetheless I shall always be grateful to the Connaught for this early hint as to the direction my theatre career should properly have taken.

Scarborough, 1998

W. Simson Fraser, later to become much better known as Bill Fraser

INTRODUCTION

'I didn't think I could do weekly rep but without my time in Worthing I wouldn't be here now,' said Patricia Routledge from the star dressing room at Brighton's Theatre Royal.

'When we left RADA in the early nineteen fifties,' recalled Roland Curram, 'we all wanted to get to Worthing. All the new talent, the actors, directors, writers and designers were coming from the Connaught Theatre.'

'Worthing was important, too important to be forgotten,' said Elizabeth Spriggs. 'From Worthing you could go anywhere, the West End, Stratford-upon-Avon, television or straight into films.'

Their colleagues in the Worthing Theatre Company in the autumn of 1956 included Alan Ayckbourn, Daniel Massey and Ian Holm, while the directors were Peter Wood and Alan Bridges. Michael Bryant had just left, Glenda Jackson and Susannah York would be arriving in a few weeks and Peter Hall had dropped in to direct a show. All of them were then unknown outside Worthing.

But it was not only in the 1950s that the Connaught Theatre played such a prominent part in the nation's theatrical life. Twenty-five years earlier, when the young Bill Fraser had established repertory in Worthing, his was one of only twenty companies outside London producing its own work throughout the year, ranking alongside Birmingham and Liverpool.

During the war the J. Arthur Rank Organisation backed the theatre as a training ground for such future stars as Robin Bailey, Diana Dors, Christopher Lee, Barbara Murray and June Whitfield. Later, when weekly repertory was no longer commercially viable, as an Arts Council-subsidised regional theatre the Connaught's fledglings included Ian Judge, David Suchet, Gwen Taylor, Susan Penhaligon, Norman Beaton, Marcus Plantin and *Star Trek*'s Marina Sertis.

Apart from Alan Ayckbourn, writers as diverse as William Douglas Home, Ray Cooney and Harold Pinter learned stagecraft at the Connaught. Even stars of opera and ballet have had their start at Worthing.

How was it that an apparently sleepy geriatric town came to have a theatre of such influence? The seeds were sown by an ambitious town council and nurtured by a Swiss piccolo player.

CHAPTER ONE

James Agate, the country's leading drama critic, was one of the first to learn, early in 1931, that Worthing was to be the home of a new repertory company. As a regular reviewer of the Independent Stage Society - a group of actors who 'tried out' new plays at West End theatres on Sunday evenings - he had seen their success in discovering works like *Journey's End* and *Young Woodley*, both of which subsequently became big money-spinners. He frequently dined with the Society's secretary, Gwladys Wheeler, and when she and a fellow member of the Society decided to form their own company it was natural that she should confide the news to Agate.

At first Wheeler had not intended to become involved in the venture; it was her partner, Walter Lindsay, who had conceived and financed the idea. They had met two years earlier when Lindsay was appointed stage manager for the London production of *Journey's End* which proved to be very lucrative for him. It was the most successful play of its time, touring all over the world. Lindsay sent out seventeen of these tours under his own management, bringing in sufficient capital to realise a growing ambition: to run a repertory company

Then in his mid-forties, Lindsay's stage career had begun carrying a spear in Beerbohm Tree's Shakespeare productions. From this he had graduated to musicals and played minor roles in several shows at the Gaiety. By 1925, however, offers of acting parts had dried up and he was forced to turn to stage management. With his newfound wealth he could return to his first love - acting. No longer would his career depend on the whims of managers, he would be in control of his own destiny.

Wheeler, on the other hand, only dabbled in the world of theatre. Her acting career had begun at the age of eighteen, with a role in the chorus of Greek women in *Hippolytus,* the production with which her close friends Harley Granville Barker and J. E. Vedrenne had opened their revolutionary season at the Court Theatre in 1906. This debut failed to lead to other roles, but Wheeler was not discouraged.

She married soon after but the relationship did not prosper and she returned to live with her mother. Divorce in those days was difficult, public and frowned upon and so she threw herself into a social life. Of independent means, she was a renowned big-game hunter, a keen rider to hounds and a regular guest at major country house parties. Her large circle of friends included Bernard Shaw, Arnold Bennett and their contemporaries; she was liked and respected by all. It was these friends who persuaded her to take over the secretaryship of the Independent Stage Society which was to prove the happiest period of her life.

Her one great regret was that she had no children.

While visiting Paris early in 1931 she was introduced to Stephen Haggard, the twenty-year-old son of Sir Godfrey Haggard, the British Chargé d'Affaires in Chicago, and a nephew of the popular author Sir Rider Haggard. The previous autumn, as he completed his studies at Munich University, he had been given a small part in a production of *Hamlet* that Max Rheinhardt, one of Europe's leading theatre directors, had put on in that city. Wheeler immediately took the young man under her wing and when he returned to England a few weeks later she introduced him to both Agate and to Nancy Price, who gave him a walk-on role in a revival of John Galsworthy's *The Silver Box* which she was putting on for a limited season at

London's Fortune Theatre. It was now that Wheeler decided to team up with Lindsay. When he had first asked her to join him she had declined, but now she undertook to throw herself whole-heartedly behind the new venture on condition that he engaged her protégé as leading juvenile. To this Lindsay agreed, even though he was already discussing a contract to play the leads with another rising young actor.

Lindsay had yet to decide where to base his company. Of the eight existing full-time repertories, seven were in the industrial north of England - which was suffering the effects of a deepening financial depression. It was while Wheeler was enjoying a weekend as a guest of Lord and Lady Leconfield at their Sussex home in Petworth that Worthing was suggested as a suitable base. The Leconfields were frequent visitors to the town where Lord Leconfield had business connections. He knew, too, that many of the members of the Borough Council were eager to promote quality entertainment in the town. The story that followed convinced Wheeler that repertory in Worthing was a distinct possibility.

Worthing, Leconfield told her, was a growing town run by a council which knew where it wanted to go. In the mid-nineteen-twenties a quarter of a million pounds had been spent on providing five hundred homes for local workers. This done, the council then set about attracting wealthy residents to the town to keep everyone in employment.

At this time party politics had not infiltrated local government: towns were run by their businessmen. Hoteliers, builders, solicitors, traders and publicans all served on local councils throughout the country. Few were in it for personal gain but they all knew, particularly in a developing area, that the more attractive they made their town the more their businesses would prosper.

Worthing is a pleasantly level coastal town with a high sunshine count in both summer and winter. At that time its population of 38,000 comprised business and professional men, the retired and the widowed. Surrounded by farms and market gardens, the profusion of grapes, tomatoes and poinsettias had earned it a name as the Madeira of England.

From early May until late October the town was packed with families on holiday - there was a daily rail service between Liverpool, Birmingham and Worthing. From November to April the plush seafront hotels were filled with retired colonels, teaplanters and ex-Indian civil servants who would stay for a month or more at a time. It was these winter visitors that the council wanted as residents.

The bucket-and-spade families were well provided for with entertainment. There were three cinemas, a new bandstand on the seafront, musical comedies at the Theatre Royal, concert parties at the Connaught Hall and at the municipally-owned pier which also housed the town's orchestra. As soon as the evenings drew in the Theatre Royal went over to cheap touring shows (usually two a week), the Connaught Hall became the home of amateur drama and dances, the bandstand and the pier pavilion closed while the municipal orchestra disbanded. The type of resident the council wanted to attract would expect a better standard of year-round entertainment and so, in June 1926, a new concert hall was opened - it was with this development in mind that the council had purchased the pier six years earlier.

Whereas the original pier pavilion was both small and perched out to sea, a quarter of a mile from the toll gate, the new concert hall could seat over 1,100 people and stood right at the pier entrance. The council had invested over £40,000 on the building, which it hoped to recoup in ten years - it did, easily. The success of the new building, however, soon created other problems: within two years the Connaught Hall had gone dark (even the amateur shows and the dances transferred to the much larger and better equipped new hall) and early in 1929 the Theatre Royal closed. The council was relieved to hear, however, that the theatre's owners had plans to alter and refurbish it and make it into a 'number one touring date' which could only enhance the town's reputation.

From the middle of May 1929 until the end of September, the new hall (now named the Pier Pavilion) housed a spectacular summer show which featured a highly popular light entertainer of the day, Rex London, and two young comediennes, Elsie and Doris Waters, who were making a big name for themselves on the new-fangled wireless: even if few people had attempted to master the 'cat's whisker' receivers, everybody read and knew about the wireless and the new stars it was creating. The Pavilion was packed; every night there were queues for returned tickets and at the end of the run the town's Entertainments Committee had made almost £2,500 from the show (which, in the 1990s would be in the region of £625,000).

But while the pier was packing them in, the Theatre Royal was lying dormant. No plans for alterations had been submitted to the Licensing Committee and, as the summer progressed, rumours began circulating that the town would have no live drama that autumn, a worry to both the local Chamber of Trade and to the council. While productions at the Theatre Royal in previous years may have been of a low standard, that there would be nothing at all in the town was unthinkable. The solution was almost revolutionary: Worthing became one of the first municipal authorities in the country to subsidise a repertory company.

Just before the summer show closed the Entertainments Committee announced that from the end of October it would run a six-week season of plays at the pier. There were to be five performances of each production, opening with a matinee on Thursday. This was a bold decision as, in the three years that the Pavilion had been open, Friday and Saturday evenings were very popular for parties and private functions; a reliable source of income was being put at risk. By not opening the productions until Thursday, however, the Monday and Wednesday tea dances, among the best supported regular events of the autumn, could continue.

Eleven players and a designer were engaged and, to compensate the amateur societies for the loss of use of the Pier Pavilion for their own productions, their members were to be asked to supplement the professionals in as many plays as possible.

On the afternoon of Thursday, 24 October 1929, the curtain went up on *Within the Law,* the first production by the Worthing Repertory Company and the first time that Worthing ratepayers had gone into show business.

The production cost £177 to stage and by Saturday night 1,795 people had paid just short of £160 to see it. Although numbers were lower than hoped for, the weather that week was atrocious. More worrying was the fact that the expensive front seats had remained empty at all performances. Prices ranged from 1/9d to 3/6d with unreserved, side seats at 1/2d. The average takings were only 1/10d per head. With the second show numbers rose to 2,233 but the average paid dropped to 1/9d: however, as this production had cost only £163 to mount there was a profit of almost £30. There was an air of optimism in the Committee and it was decided, providing public support was maintained, to extend the season through until Easter.

The first six productions were seen by 12,200 people who paid a total of £1,035 at the box office. Although expenses had run out at £1,064 the council declared it was happy to suffer a loss of £29 in view of the entertainment that the company was providing for the town. This support was not of, course, unanimous. One councillor pointed out that during the same period the previous year £74 had been earned by letting the pavilion for private functions; another countered that as they had acquired scenery and fittings worth about £130 this more than outweighed the loss on both the lettings and the repertory season to date. But it was made clear to the public that if it wanted the repertory to stay its support must be unwavering even in the event of a hard winter.

In all, nineteen productions were staged (including the British premiere of a Broadway success, *Freddy*) but the season resulted in a loss of £213, sufficient for the council to declare that it would not be staging a second season, even if the Theatre Royal failed to reopen.

As soon as she returned to London, Wheeler reported this story to Lindsay. He knew the town, having played at the Theatre Royal on occasions. As far as he was concerned, however, the action of the council was not quite the deciding factor: two years earlier a repertory company had set up in Folkestone for just six weeks - now its season lasted from Easter to Christmas. With its wealthy, retired population, Worthing was a similar type of town. Being seaside resorts both had an influx of visitors for the summer months which would be a reliable source of income to a theatre in its early days.

During the winter of 1931, as the *Worthing Gazette* began a regular column on the latest invention, television, Worthing's theatregoers either watched the local amateurs or went to Brighton for their entertainment. But it did seem they would soon have top-class productions on their doorstep since plans for the reconstruction of the Theatre Royal as an 'elegant playhouse seating 1,900' had received the council's approval.

Lindsay started negotiations for a lease on the theatre but after much procrastination the owners told him that the reconstruction plans had been abandoned and that the Theatre Royal would remain closed for the foreseeable future. All the more reason, thought Lindsay, to be in Worthing.

He at once contacted Carl Seebold, the owner of the only other suitable building in the town, the Connaught Hall. The Hall had been dark for two years, so Seebold was delighted to get the place off his hands - and at the end of March Lindsay signed a twelve months' lease with the option to renew.

The Connaught Hall had opened in October 1916. Built above a parade of shops in one of the town's main roads it was adjacent to the Picturedrome cinema, also owned by Seebold. The hall was originally designed as a meeting place for lectures, recitals and whist drives but, following a dearth of bookings during its first winter, in the following summer it had housed a succession of touring concert parties, briefly taking the name the 'Vaudeville Theatre'.

Its two dressing rooms were on either side of the small stage, perched high above the wing space. Each, barely 130 square feet in area, was reached by a rickety ladder. The audience sat on hard-backed chairs and the general atmosphere was what could be expected in a hall opened by a meeting of the Brotherhood and addressed by the editor of the *Christian World Pulpit.*

Lindsay realised the hall was not ideal, but thought that with redecoration and a little alteration it could be converted into an intimate theatre for about 500, though the stage would be cramped. Friends in the London theatre world were called on to lend a hand and at the beginning of April a small army invaded the Connaught. The floor of the balcony was raised, new stage lighting installed and what had once been a kitchen was converted into a lounge bar. The hard, upright chairs, however, remained in the stalls and somehow the hoped-for intimate atmosphere was not captured.

A company of six men and three women was engaged for the season, one of the actors doubling as set designer, while Lindsay himself would combine playing leading roles with directing productions. All the men, with the exception of Stephen Haggard, had worked with Lindsay on his *Journey's End* tours and one brought along his wife to play juvenile leads. They were a friendly gang but, unfortunately, none of them had any experience of the rigours of staging a different play every week.

The opening night was set for Saturday, 25 April 1931. It had been Lindsay's original intention to open with John Van Druten's much talked-of drama, *Young Woodley,* with another of his *Journey's End* colleagues, Terence de Marney, in the title role: this was the actor Lindsay was having discussions with when Gwladys Wheeler brought Haggard on to the scene. Then only twenty-two, de Marney was already making a name for himself in London circles as actor, manager and dramatist. In Worthing he was to be a prominent member of the company as well as personal assistant to Lindsay and director of some productions. However, a sudden offer of film work prevented him joining the company immediately, so Lindsay had to change his plans. *Art and Mrs. Bottle*, a comedy by Benn W. Levy which had met with considerable success in London a couple of years earlier, was chosen as the opening piece with Stephen Haggard in the lead.

During her preliminary investigation of Worthing, Wheeler had concluded it was a town of intellectual snobs and so she announced that the first night audience would include R. C. Sherriff and John Van Druten, respectively authors of *Journey's End* and *Young Woodley*, together with the renowned novelist H. G. Wells and, of course, James Agate. Like Lord and Lady Leconfield, all of them, unfortunately, turned out to have prior engagements, but the Mayor and Mayoress of Worthing were official guests amongst an audience of three hundred.

When the two local papers appeared the following week their reviews were guarded but they could not overlook the stage management problems, the several prompts and some indifferent acting. They were, however, unstinting in their praise for the young Haggard.

After the opening night the advance booking was not great and few tickets were sold at the door. Prices were high, ranging from 1/2d to 5/9d (6p - 28p): at this time the top price at the local cinemas for the latest releases was 1/9d and at the Pier Pavilion for a top-name light entertainer, 3/6d.

In view of the number of company members who had been associated with the play, it was inevitable that *Journey's End* should be one of the very early productions and for this Lindsay called in his first guest player, Cyril Gardener, who had taken over the leading role of Stanhope during the London run. Although the film version had been a great success in the town, this was the first time that the play had been seen in Worthing, yet audiences were sparse.

In another letter to Agate, Wheeler admitted that although they were not doing as well as they had hoped she was convinced that a repertory theatre in Worthing should succeed, 'but it's hard work getting it going. The Worthingites are very conservative and want to be quite sure that they are doing the right thing before they patronise a new venture! I feel that if I could get a few words in the best London papers about our work it would do us an infinite amount of good, more than any advertising in the local papers or by posters.'

An ardent follower of the 'progressive' school of acting and writing, Gwladys Wheeler's avowed aim was to convert the British public to the joys of great drama. She wanted the Worthing Repertory Company to follow Barry Jackson's Birmingham Rep in producing the works of Strindberg, Chekhov and Shakespeare. For this she needed the backing of an intellectual audience which could be stimulated by a society which would study and debate the finest works of dramatic literature.

When, a few days later, she announced the formation of the Worthing Stage Society, *The Times* reported that Somerset Maugham, Sybil Thorndike, John Gielgud and Athene Seyler had shown interest and would all be addressing meetings. None of them, in fact, were at the three which were held, although Maurice Browne, who had staged *Journey's End*, attended the inauguration of the Society. Worthing theatregoers, however intellectual, were indeed conservative and were not inclined to pay an annual subscription of 10/6d to foster Greek tragedy and Nordic doom: so few turned up to that first meeting in July. Unfortunately for the Connaught, the new Society and particularly for Lindsay, Wheeler, who did not enjoy the best of health, was taken seriously ill and forced to abandon Worthing soon afterward.

In their fourth week Terence de Marney arrived. Met at the station by the press, he declared that the company was going to make the Connaught so much a part of Worthing that it would be seriously missed if it went. Backstage that night it was a very different story.

De Marney was in the audience for the opening night of *Interference*. He was horrified at what he saw: lines were fluffed, cues and entrances missed, the prompter was heard as often as the leading man, the set was appalling, the show totally under-rehearsed and the ticket prices were far too high.

When, eventually, de Marney had finished with him after the show Lindsay felt punch-drunk. Reluctantly he had to accept de Marney's ultimatum, an ultimatum he could ill afford: if he was to stay the company must be enlarged to allow two weeks' rehearsal, an experienced designer must be appointed and the ticket prices must immediately be reduced to the same level as those at the Pier Pavilion.

The next day de Marney returned to London to engage more actors. His diagnosis of the problems proved right - there was an immediate improvement in the standards. But the damage had been done: people who had been once were not impressed, they did not return and they told their friends why. The local press, however, was very supportive, with free advertising and plenty of editorial praise for the venture if not always for the productions.

Then came more setbacks: Terence de Marney left after five frustrating weeks and Stephen Haggard, who had been first class in every role he had played, departed in order to go to the Royal Academy of Dramatic Art.

The world outside the theatre was going through hard times. Unemployment figures were rising and many of those who were fortunate enough to be in work were having to take cuts in income: the country was in the throes of a financial crisis. Lindsay was a man of theatre, not a man of business, and without Wheeler he was lost. He knew audiences were small, takings were poor and that only four of the twenty-two productions staged had made a profit, but he was astounded when, on 30 September, he was summoned to his bank manager's desk. His credit was exhausted.

Bewildered, he turned to everyone he thought might be able to help him. He went to the Borough Council but all local authorities had been told by the Treasury to reduce expenditure; furthermore Worthing had burnt its fingers once before on repertory and that mistake was not going to be repeated (the fact that the council was about to plough £190 into an amateur production of an opera written by the director of the Municipal Orchestra was tactfully ignored!

On Monday, 5 October, the curtain went up as usual; but in the programme for *The Thief* by Cosmo Gordon Lang, there was no mention of the following week's attraction. Throughout the week Lindsay had been in touch with friends and possible partners but by 6.30 that Saturday evening he had exhausted all his contacts with no more solid results than vague promises for the future. He was facing the final performance of his Worthing Repertory Company - no need for an option to renew his lease. Although the local press had not liked *The Thief* ('not a good play but the Connaught company made the best of a very bad job') the *Worthing Herald* predicted that 'the closing of the Connaught will be a greater loss to Worthing than it may possibly realise at the moment.'

If the second Worthing Repertory Company had failed it set a precedent which its successors followed: the promotion of outstanding talent.

In Stephen Haggard it had given experience of the English stage to an actor soon to be hailed as one of the most outstanding young players of the day and who, but for his death in 1943, might well have become one of the country's greatest actors. After leaving Worthing he went to drama school for a year; when he made his London debut in *The Laughing Woman* at the New Theatre in April, 1934, one critic referred to him as 'a young actor with true genius in him'. For Haggard himself that occasion was marred by the death of Gwladys Wheeler just hours before the curtain went up. 'If I hadn't met Gwladys Wheeler,' he wrote to his mother, 'I should never have got on the English stage at all.'

Five years after his appearances at the Connaught he played Constantin in Komisarjevsky's famous production of *The Seagull* with John Gielgud, Edith Evans and Peggy Ashcroft. His last performance was as the Fool to Gielgud's *King Lear* at the Old Vic in April, 1940.

Leslie Sands, who later built up a big following at the Connaught, recalled being taken to see *Candida* in 1935 at the age of fourteen: 'one day it would dawn on me that I had been privileged to witness Stephen Haggard's unrivalled portrayal of Marchbanks.'

For Walter Lindsay Worthing was not quite journey's end: he did re-establish himself as an actor and returned to the West End, playing supporting roles in several plays by Ivor Novello.

The Connaught was dark. The only live professional entertainment in the town, apart from the Municipal Orchestra (whose future was also in the balance), was the Saturday variety shows at the Pier Pavilion and even these were discontinued early in 1932 through lack of support. Between Easter and Whitsun a few of Worthing's theatre enthusiasts would take the train to Brighton (steam driven still, the lines from Worthing had yet to be electrified) where Terence Duff was presenting his Phoenix Players for a six-week season at the Palace Pier Theatre. They had a successful run and would have gone on longer but for a previous booking at the theatre. Their season had to end on Saturday, 14 May, but the company was offered a return engagement from the middle of June.

Four weeks to kill and a vacant theatre only ten miles away! Despite a growing feeling within the profession that Worthing was not theatre-minded, Duff decided to risk a couple of weeks at the Connaught.

The Phoenix Players was one of the many touring repertory companies of the time, a small group of actors playing perhaps a fortnight here followed by six or eight weeks at the next engagement. A repertoire of small cast, popular plays that could be staged efficiently and inexpensively. Occasionally the length of stay in a town would warrant the expense of enlarging the company temporarily. Terence Duff and his wife, Ruth Robinson, led the group and one of their chief stalwarts was Malcolm Tearle, brother of the renowned actor, Godfrey Tearle.

The Connaught run opened with Frederick Lonsdale's *On Approval*, always popular with audiences, and Monday saw a very good house which was kept up throughout the week. For the second production *Fallen Angels* by Noel Coward was staged and again business was good, even though both plays had just been done in Brighton. During the second week, too, they had been up against fierce competition from the Pier Pavilion where Ben Greet and his company were playing a Shakespeare season. Also during this fortnight the 'wireless' had come into full flower with its move from Savoy Hill to Broadcasting House, so more people had been buying receivers and were tempted to stay at home listening to the improved programmes. Continual touring was all very well but it was a wearing and unsettled life; for some time Duff had been looking for somewhere to settle permanently or at least find a base of a long winter season: it began to look as though Worthing might be the answer. He decided that the two remaining weeks before the return to Brighton would be spent in Worthing. Tentatively, he let it be known that he might return to the town at the end of the summer for an indefinite period. The response was positive and he began to plan for the future.

The Connaught remained closed during the four weeks that the Phoenix Players were at Brighton, but Duff returned to Worthing for another fortnight before setting off on a long-planned three months' tour of Wales and the Midlands. During his stay in Brighton he had negotiated a lease on the Connaught and he then engaged several touring productions to keep the theatre occupied until the Phoenix Players could return in the autumn. He delegated his company manager, Charles W. Bell, to look after the Connaught in the interim.

Bell had begun his life in the theatre ten years earlier in stage management but after a while he turned to the business side, becoming manager to a succession of itinerant companies such as Duff's. He had not the slightest idea how this short assignment would change his career.

The first of the touring shows, *Mary's Other Husband*, which arrived on 18 July 1932, was headed by one of the most popular stage and film stars of the day, Renée Kelly. The play had been a success on Broadway and was now en route to London. It was topical, about life in the world of cinema, and taking the leading male role was Renée Kelly's handsome husband, Hylton Allen. It surely could not fail to draw the crowds. However the first night audience was depressingly small and despite the *Worthing Herald* declaring that 'the show is a winner all the way and should make a big hit in town,' the theatre remained virtually empty for the whole week. The touring season was off to a bad start and so it continued.

Although the touring companies were losing money, when Duff returned as a guest of Worthing Rotary Club meeting on 22 August he spoke of his plans to present a competent company in recent West End plays when the Phoenix Players returned to the Connaught in October. He even promised 'a little Shakespeare at times'.

Bell, however, sensed that Duff was having second thoughts and, with permission, took a week's leave from the Connaught to look after the Lyric Theatre, Hammersmith, while the resident manager was on holiday. Being in London would give him an opportunity to check out what other jobs in his line were on offer.

The last of the tours was scheduled for the week of the 9th October then the theatre was to be given over to an exhibition for a week, but what next? Duff had not given an actual date for the return of his company and there was even a rumour that the Connaught was going over to twice-nightly entertainment: this could only mean variety - surely not Worthing's cup of tea!

Then the announcement was made. 'After being closed for redecoration the Connaught Theatre will re-open on Monday, 24 October, 1932, when Charles W. Bell and W. Simson Fraser will present the Mask Players in a season of repertory productions.'

The overture was done, the beginners had left the stage, the action was about to start.

CHAPTER TWO

Whilst chatting to a friend in the bar of the Lyric, Bell was introduced to W. Simson Fraser.

'Call me Bill,' was Fraser's opening remark. 'I only use the other name professionally - W. Simson Fraser looks so much more imposing on the posters than plain Bill Fraser.'

Fraser was twenty-four, eleven years younger than Bell, and he was celebrating the completion of his first year as a professional actor. Born and brought up in the Scottish town of Perth, his first job was in a bank but he did not enjoy the routine and soon left to work in his father's tweed retailing business.

It was the theatre, though, that was his real love and inevitably before long he decided to become an actor. Initially his parents, who were very comfortably off, disapproved of the move but when his first year turned out to be busy, disapproval became pride.

Within two days of arriving in London - and two nights sleeping on the Embankment - he was offered a part in a show in Broadstairs. That was immediately followed by a long tour of India and Asia and, although he was out of work at the moment, he was contracted for a six-week tour of the West Indies over Christmas. What he really wanted to do, though, was to run his own company, pick the plays, cast all the roles and produce the shows as he thought they should be done. In his mind he had already decided that his company would be called the Mask Players, and he knew a couple of actors he thought were good enough for him to employ.

Bell took an instant liking to this ebullient young man with his supreme confidence, accompanied by a generosity of spirit and a contagious laugh. Over several large whiskies Bell talked about Worthing and his doubts that Duff and his small company would make a success of the Connaught. Within weeks the railway line to London would be electrified, bringing a faster and more comfortable journey to the West End.

To succeed at the Connaught productions would have to be up to London standards, nothing could appear cheap. The plays must be current successes, well acted and, above all, expertly designed and staged. He conceded that the theatre was not ideal but he had ideas for its improvement which would include raking the stalls and renewing all the seating.

Bell and Fraser's ideas of the standards which a repertory company should reach were identical. If Duff did throw in the towel why shouldn't they go into partnership - it seemed that what one didn't know about theatre the other did? They parted that night full of ideas and hope.

They were in contact again as soon as Duff confirmed to Bell his decision to abandon the Worthing plan. Less than a week after their first meeting Bell and Fraser had become partners and an appointment was made to discuss terms with the Connaught's owner, Carl Seebold.

Seebold, the youngest son in a large family of Swiss musicians, was a very astute businessman and one of Worthing's major property owners. Born in 1873, he was just five years old when he joined the family band as its piccolo player. They had managed to eke a living by playing in the cafes of St. Maurice and Martigny, but their fortunes changed a year after Carl joined the group when two wealthy Englishmen holidaying in the area heard the ensemble and engaged them for one of the major balls of the London season. Carl and his sisters were left in Switzerland with their mother, but the male section of the band made so great an impression in London that their stay was prolonged and they were engaged for many major social events, including playing in the royal enclosure at race meetings.

Three years later the Seebold family had made such a success in England that they uprooted from their native land and made their home in London. Soon they were playing regularly throughout the nation and on one occasion gave a Command Performance for Queen Victoria at Balmoral.

Following the sudden deaths of both his father and his eldest brother the family elected Carl as their leader when he was twenty-four. Two years later he made a very shrewd move when he took a five-year lease on Southend's pier pavilion, where they played each summer. By the time the lease came to an end Carl had both a gold watch from the grateful mayor and town councillors and a very substantial bank balance. He also had ambitions beyond being a bandleader.

As they prepared to leave Southend in 1904 Worthing's Theatre Royal came on the market. The band had performed in the town several times and were always well received. Carl bought the theatre, which he ran for over fifteen years with varying degrees of fortune. It was diversification into other forms of entertainment, however, that multiplied his wealth.

Before the First World War he developed a site on the seafront as a roller-skating rink-cum-concert hall capable of seating 3,000. Above it was to be a ballroom but days before it was due to open in 1911 he decided, instead, to use the space as a cinema.

Soon he realised that far more money was to be made out of the silent, flickering shadows than from live entertainment and, apart from Christmas and the summer months, films occupied the Theatre Royal more often than stage shows for much of his regime.

On 29 July 1914, just a week before the outbreak of the First World War, Worthing's first purpose-built cinema, the 860-seater Picturedrome, opened. It was an instant triumph and within six years its founders had recovered all their outlay plus a profit of about 25%. When peace was restored Seebold decided to mount an all-out attack on this rival.

First he converted his roller-skating rink into the Dome luxury cinema, then he sold the Theatre Royal and built another cinema, the Rivoli, which, with 1,700 seats, opened in 1924. His aim was achieved the following year when the Picturedrome, now in dire straits, came into his control. Three cinemas in the town and he owned them all.

By this time Seebold had no need of, or faith in, theatre. When he took over the Picturedrome the Connaught Hall came with it, but as far as he was concerned it was an encumbrance - though he wouldn't have minded a regular income from it.

Like everyone else, when Seebold first met Fraser he was impressed by his confidence. After an hour spent exploring the theatre Fraser saw clearly what had to be done to create a better atmosphere. The place needed redecorating and, Bell had been right, new seating was needed, the rear stalls had to be raked, also, he felt, by painting the proscenium black and replacing the the footlights and battens by spotlights fixed in the auditorium, they could concentrate the audience's attention on the stage picture.

Seebold listened carefully to Fraser's ideas for the alterations and to his plans for the plays he proposed to stage. Resources would be tight, but Fraser so convinced Seebold that success was inevitable that a pleasantly low initial rental was agreed.

Seebold told his new tenants that as the Theatre Royal was about to go into liquidation they might be able to pick up much of the equipment they would need for next to nothing. He also offered a little financial support by undertaking to advertise his cinemas in the theatre's programmes.

They would be able to put on six productions before Fraser started rehearsals for the West Indies tour and the partners calculated that, including the cost of alterations, they would need £600 to set themselves up. Bell could provide £250 of this immediately.

With his usual charm and confidence, Fraser was able to talk his father into putting up the balance. It was not only financial support that Alexander Fraser gave to the venture: he and his wife, Bettie, decided to take time off from the business and come down to Worthing to man the box office.

One thing Fraser realised was the need for publicity and the value of a 'story', something he put to good use on many occasions.

Confidence in themselves was of paramount importance, even if it did mean the odd white lie. In the first, smart brochure he boasted: 'I take the greatest pride in presenting to you the Mask Players because in this topsy-turvey world of entertainment, they have won through and are acknowledged to be one of the finest repertory companies in England' - all this before they had even set foot on any stage!

The rumour that the Connaught was going over to twice-nightly entertainment was not unfounded, for the brochure did indeed announce that there would be two performances each evening, one at 6.30 and the second at 8.45. Some repertory companies then running, such as Northampton and the Alexandra in Birmingham, operated on a twice-nightly basis, arguing that this reduced seat prices to cinema levels and, at the same time, increased revenue sufficiently to employ a cast large enough to allow the leading players to have every third or fourth week off.

On the other hand it limited the choice of plays that could be produced: most three-act plays of the time ran for at least two hours twenty minutes which meant that substantial cuts had to be made to accommodate them within the twice-nightly repertory time scale, cuts which many of the most popular and successful playwrights refused to allow. The very plays that Fraser thought would draw in an audience were ruled out by their length. Almost at the last moment Bell and Fraser changed their minds and opted, instead, for one performance per night with a matinee on Wednesdays, the local early closing day.

When news of their plans broke in theatrical circles everybody scoffed. Fancy two young men throwing their money away in Worthing of all places - everyone knew it was a graveyard: just you ask Walter Lindsay!

Undeterred, they pressed on. *By Candlelight*, which had just ended a year's run at the Prince of Wales Theatre, was chosen as the opening production. But so much needed doing and there was so little time. Bell concentrated on supervising the alterations while Fraser was busy organising the company and rehearsing. Within a week everything was ready for curtain up.

A company of eight had been engaged, one of whom, Robert Metcalfe, doubled as designer. Although originally he had proposed to direct the productions himself, at the last moment Fraser recruited Clive Woods, an experienced actor, as the principal director.

A rather thin comedy, *By Candlelight* is about a baron's valet who, in his absence, impersonates his master and entertains a lady to dinner: the baron, of course, returns unexpectedly. Fraser played the baron with Clive Woods as the valet and

Ethel Hope-Johnstone as the lady. In supporting roles were Beryl Measor and Raymond Francis, the two young actors Fraser knew he wanted to employ.

The proceeds of the first night, just over £25, were to go to Worthing Hospital which gave the evening an air of occasion even if the theatre was not full. The show went well, the audience seemed to enjoy it and the new lighting was very effective, particularly in the scenes which were apparently played in candlelight. The *Worthing Herald* described Fraser's performance as 'exceedingly good' and noted as an unusual feature that the subsidiary roles were played as though they were as important as the leads.

In his curtain speech Fraser promised to give Worthing some really good plays and hoped to include some by Shaw and Galsworthy. *Flat to Let*, the latest comedy success by Arthur Macrae, was the following week's attraction and the Connaught was to be one of the first repertory theatres to stage it.

Realising that judging public taste is difficult, each playgoer that week was given a list of various types of plays and asked to indicate his preferences. The local press commended the idea, having often noticed that the tastes of residents differed greatly from those of holidaymakers. Young audiences, too, were to be encouraged and the local branch of the Junior Imperial League was invited to become associated with the Connaught to enjoy back-stage tours and reduced price tickets.

Flat to Let was not liked by the press but both local papers thought it was well staged. Audiences, however, were meagre. The first serious drama, *Outward Bound,* received excellent notices: the *Worthing Gazette,* not always noted for praise, wrote: 'it is produced in a far finer way than one dares to expect or even hope for in any provincial theatre.'

As trial runs of the new electric trains to London and Brighton began, the Connaught staged *The Ghost Train*, which had not only enjoyed a hugely successful London run but had been filmed and published as a book. To ensure that the complicated effects were up to standard a technical director was hired for this production. Although the press described the show as 'spine chilling', Bill Fraser's own notices were bad. He played the role of a silly ass, and one critic wrote that had he tried less hard to be funny he would have been funnier while the other declared he had no conception of the part.

As planned, the season ended after six weeks so that Fraser could undertake his West Indies tour but Worthing was told that the company was going to Manchester.

Bell and Fraser found, as had Gwladys Wheeler, that Worthing was wary of anything new and at the end of the six weeks their initial £600 had almost vanished; but they were determined they were not going to pack up yet.

In Fraser's eyes the first season was not only a financial failure but an artistic one, too. Although he was satisfied with *By Candlelight* and *The Ghost Train* he felt the other four productions were below par. This he blamed on Clive Woods, who had directed them. He was sure that his worries about the direction were affecting his own performances - he knew he should have been very much better in *The Ghost Train* and agreed with the press comments. What was the point in employing a director whose work was not up to scratch?

More money had to be found - Fraser was determined to show Worthing what good acting and good direction were and he would provide both himself. Alexander and Bettie Fraser still strongly supported their son and his partner but during their time in the box office they had seen little money coming in. They agreed that six weeks was far too short a time to judge whether the venture could be turned into a success and were quite amenable to putting up more capital. Bell, however, was strongly opposed to this; he felt they should be confident enough to raise money from outside sources and undertook to look for backers whilst Fraser was away.

Meanwhile the parents returned to Scotland, ready to come south again should their help be needed. As it turned out no more help was required but they decided to retire from their business and moved to a house in Christchurch Road, Worthing, later in 1933 where they remained until their deaths in the 1950s.

New companies were sprouting like mushrooms, often led by young actors unable to get any other work. A newly married couple, Geoffrey Bragg and Laura Liddell, both in their early twenties, had, like Fraser, borrowed from their parents. Their plans were to tour a repertoire of classic and modern plays through Scotland, setting off in January. Bell suggested that they should come to the Connaught for a trial run in the three weeks prior to Christmas.

They did six plays in the three weeks, four by Shakespeare, *She Stoops to Conquer* and a contemporary piece by A. A. Milne, *Michael and Mary*. As might be expected at that time of the year and with that type of repertoire, they played to depressingly small houses and lost most of their money - in the final week their total takings were £18.

The newly-weds fought on, however, and later, when Geoffrey Bragg changed his surname to Kendal his company's tours of India became legendary. Geoffrey Kendal became the internationally known 'Shakespeare Wallah' and subject of the film.

Following a week of pantomime (which grossed £394) Bell let the theatre to Reginald Newson and Rex Thackeray who ran another of those touring repertories. It remained uncertain how long it would take to raise sufficient capital for the Mask Players to return: the terms of their occupancy were that they could stay until either side gave two weeks' notice.

Bell decided that it would be difficult to find finance in Worthing and so, once again, headed for London. There he was introduced to Leslie Stocker, a wealthy, retired man who enjoyed mixing with theatre people. He had been an 'angel', investing in West End productions but he had never before been approached to back a provincial repertory company. Stocker came to Worthing, liked the little theatre and met Seebold who still maintained his faith in the Mask Players. On his return from the West Indies, Fraser was introduced, but this time his confidence did not win him everything he wanted.

Stocker agreed to give the Players some help, but in return he was to become their General Manager. He expressed the view that neither Bell nor Fraser was sufficiently experienced in business matters although his real aim was probably to create an interest for himself. Bell was to run the theatre, with Fraser responsible for what went on the stage; both were agreeable to this. A second condition, however, was more worrying. Stocker would finance the company for three productions at a time but could pull out and cut his losses by giving just three weeks' notice. Bell was not happy with these terms; Fraser, with his usual insouciance, was unconcerned.

Newman and Thackeray were told that their fifth production would have to be their last, but in view of their short stay Fraser suggested that they should join forces with the Mask Players for one week to present *The Trial of Mary Dugan* with a cast of thirty. Stocker's finances were not required for this production and, despite their own losses, they gave a special Saturday matinee performance in aid of the local unemployed which raised £20.

Much of the country was in the grip of depression, but, though there was unemployment in the town, Worthing was sheltered from the worst ravages of the 'hungry thirties'. Indeed, the town was beginning to expand even more rapidly. New properties were being built in the desirable Charmandean area, where a four-bedroom house cost as much as £1,650 - a considerable sum compared to £125 for a new Austin Seven or the latest radio set at £18. (All these, of course, were beyond the reach of the average man whose wage was about £200 a year.) The Connaught's charges of 9d to 3/-d (4p to 15p) compared well with cinema prices which ranged from 9d - 2/6d and were not too outrageous when compared with the cost of a three-course meal at 1/9d.

After *The Trial of Mary Dugan* the Mask Players were on their own again. This time the company was increased in numbers from eight to fourteen with Raymond Francis and Beryl Measor returning to the Connaught and four of the Newson/Thackeray company staying on in Worthing. This time, too, a set designer, Daniel Barker, who had worked on several London productions, was engaged. Three plays were advertised, but all did badly although a couple of letters in the local press praised the acting and urged more support for the theatre.

While Bell was worried, Stocker was already becoming frightened: his money was going out far quicker than he had anticipated. He had not appreciated the problems of running a provincial repertory theatre.

The Connaught was not untypical in having an average of fourteen acting members whose wages totalled around £80 a week; backstage and front-of-house staff cost a further £40, while rents, rates scenery and advertising took the outgoings to about £150. With a full house the box office could take around £42 a night from which had to be deducted the crippling Entertainment Tax of almost 16% - this had been introduced in 1916 as a temporary measure - and the author's royalties which, for a popular writer, would be 10%. Seven full houses a week would produce a profit of around £65, plus profits from the sale of programmes and bar takings. If attendances dropped to only 50% the loss for the week would hit almost £50 and so far there had not been a single night on which they had managed to sell half the tickets.

Stocker told the partners that unless there was an upturn he would exercise his option to pull out: three more productions was all he was prepared to sponsor. Fraser dismissed the worries. What concerned him was, in his view, much more serious: how to present a high-class production with an acting area less than twelve feet deep and twenty-two feet wide. There was no room above to 'fly' scenery and the wing space was minimal. Some companies, such as the one at Richmond in Surrey - which had much better facilities - used only painted backcloths and curtains, but Fraser and his designer, Daniel Barker, demanded a realistic decor. Fortunately they had rented a garage below the theatre where they could construct and paint the sets, manoeuvring them up the narrow staircase after the final curtain every Saturday night.

Despite the problems, Fraser was determined that their next production, *Pygmalion* with its three enormous sets and a cast of eighteen, was to be as good as anything that could be seen in the West End. His confidence as a director was building up and he had no qualms at both playing the role of Higgins and directing the production.

When the brochure for the second set of three plays was published nobody would have realised the company was facing any problems at all. 'May we take the opportunity of thanking you for your support this Spring Season,' wrote Fraser. 'We are fast making more and more friends in Worthing. As a natural result of this the more friends we make the better will be the shows we present to you. At last Worthing seems to be waking up to the fact that a real theatre presenting up-to-date shows in an up-to-date manner is on their doorstep.... The company has had two offers to go to big theatres for seasons, but we have turned them down preferring rather to stay in our own theatre in Worthing.'

Because of its length (three hours) *Pygmalion* began half-an-hour earlier and there was an extra matinee on Saturday afternoon. Monday night saw a larger audience than usual and during the following day the box office was kept quite busy. By the end of the week the response was definitely encouraging and there was a small profit. At last, with their eleventh home-grown production, a glimmer of hope. The next week *Hay Fever* played to even better business and *On the Spot* which followed it showed a very satisfactory profit. Stocker was smiling broadly, all talk of pulling out was silenced. Suddenly it seemed his 'boys' could have anything they wanted. Fraser could not understand the fuss: hadn't he said all along that success was inevitable?

During the first week of April the Mask Players gave their 100th performance at the Connaught and the *Worthing Gazette* commented: 'to have confounded the pessimists by keeping the flag of drama proudly flying... is an achievement of which the management may be justly proud. Well done the Connaught and the Mask Players. May you now begin to reap your reward.' And, indeed, they did.

News that the Connaught shows were worth seeing spread rapidly and just six weeks after *Pygmalion* they staged Shaw's *St. Joan* - marred by some poor speaking and too much doubling of characters which was confusing. This was followed by the first repertory production of *Autumn Crocus* which was so successful that it was retained for a second week, showing a profit of £197. Before long matinees were being given on both Wednesdays and Saturdays.

Despite the small stage and lack of technical facilities Bell and Fraser undertook adventurous productions, often using large casts and several sets. The standard they set was high and when, that summer, the *Sunday Referee* sent a critic round the country to compare all the repertory companies then operating, Worthing was given a very high rating - only Bristol and Edinburgh were considered of a higher standard, and both of these had been in existence for considerably more than nine months.

When in October 1933 they staged *The Barretts of Wimpole Street* (another production that had to be retained for a second week), its author, Rudolph Besier, wrote to Fraser, 'My wife thought your performance of *The Barretts* among the very best she has ever seen and, including the London production, she must have seen half a dozen different companies.... I wish I had been able to see the performance myself.' Perhaps he might also have liked to watch the ladies of the cast clambering down the ladder from the dressing room displaying their bloomers before stepping into their voluminous crinolines at the side of the stage.

On 23 October 1933, exactly a year after the opening night, Alexander and Bettie Fraser, together with Leslie Stocker, were guests of honour at a celebration party after the show. The whisky flowed and, for once, Charles Bell was in almost as ebullient a mood as Bill Fraser. It had been a triumphant year and that morning they had repaid all their debts. From now on the partners were running their own business and Bell was once again General Manager. Today they had greeted their audience with a much smarter and better printed programme and instead of records providing the interval music there was a live orchestra.

It had been a busy year for Fraser: he had directed 29 of their 34 productions and appeared in 30 of them. Most of the plays had been West End successes but they had also given the premiere of a new play by Cecile Adair, a local writer - and it, like the others, had made a profit!

A lot can happen in a year and Bell had been proved right: a good company doing up-to-the-minute plays did appeal to Worthing audiences.

If it was a good year for Bell and Fraser it had been a worrying time for their landlord. Designs for two new cinemas soon to be built in the town were revealed. Each was to seat over 2,500 and have facilities for staging lavish shows. The 'talkies' had arrived five years earlier; now it looked as though cine-variety, the latest craze in London, was about to hit Worthing.

The usual pattern for cinema programmes was a feature film supported by a 'B' movie, the news, a cartoon and a short 'interest' item. London's cinemas were pulling in huge audiences with just the feature film accompanied by a song-and-dance show, each lasting about an hour and a half. With the depression getting deeper people wanted glamour as a relief but it had to come cheap. As the film was the main attraction the glamour could be provided without the expense of a big star, all at normal cinema prices.

If that was the way Worthing was going Seebold resolved to be ready for it. Of his three cinemas the smallest, the Picturedrome, was most suitable for expansion and much as Seebold disliked the idea of going back to live shows, if that was what was needed he would be prepared.

In May 1933, just as Bell and Fraser had begun to turn the corner, the Picturedrome closed for twelve weeks. In that time the auditorium was extended, a stage, fly tower and dressing rooms were built and a safety curtain installed - rescued, like the Connaught's lighting, from the Theatre Royal. The cinema was completely redecorated and refurbished. As it happened, Seebold need not have worried: the new cinemas did not attempt cine-variety nor did the alterations to the Picturedrome secure its future as a cinema. But the investment was not wasted.

There was no let-up in the work going on at the Connaught though the company no longer had a corporate name. After paying off their debts, the partners dropped the

Autumn Crocus, *staged in 1933, was so successful that, for the first time, the run was extended by a week. Playing the harp is Bill Fraser*

The Mask Players taking a curtain call in The Barretts of Wimpole Street, *another production that had its run extended*

'Mask Players' label. The cast were usually referred to as 'Bell and Fraser's people', or sometimes the press called them 'The Connaught Theatre Repertory Company'. It was not until a year later they became the Worthing Repertory Company.

That November came a challenging play, *Children in Uniform*. It had a large all-female cast and ten settings while the story had strong hints of lesbianism - a real challenge, one would have thought, in a town like Worthing. A few months later came *The Green Bay Tree* in which the homosexual theme was even more overt. Both plays were well received by large audiences without a murmur of disapproval. (Forty years later, when plays of this nature were staged in Worthing there was to be uproar in the local press!)

With the success of the Connaught established Bell and Fraser thought they should take a more active part in the social life of the town. At Christmas they wrote and staged a pantomime, *Aladdin*, which ran for three weeks (being gluttons for punishment, they re-wrote the script, incorporating new gags, scenes and songs for the third week to keep the show 'fresh'!) They filled the theatre at the dress rehearsal with 475 children from needy families and talked the local Rotary Club into providing buns and sweets for the youngsters while the Mayoress was persuaded to see that every child was given an orange to take home.

Not content with this, they organised a 'Panto Ball' at which the cast, after a full day in the theatre, provided the cabaret. Held at a local hotel, it drew a large crowd and raised a substantial sum for the local hospital.

Too late they realised they were over-working the company when the leading lady, Ethel Hope-Johnstone, suffered a nervous breakdown as rehearsals for the pantomime were getting under way and had to be replaced. For the next couple of years they let an outside management put on the Christmas show to give the repertory players a break. The 'Panto Ball' was then replaced by a 'Repertory Ball' which became one of the most eagerly awaited events of the autumn season. In the summer there were Sunday outings to Windsor or Henley-on-Thames enjoyed by the company, theatre staff and Worthing residents filling three and, sometimes, four fifty-seater coaches.

The cast had a second break in August when a touring show was brought in for a week. This meant that the regular players had one week with no rehearsals and the second with no evening performances and no pay - wages in the theatre were for performing, not rehearsing.

Some of the regular patrons felt after a while that the applause at curtain fall was not an adequate way of thanking Bell and Fraser for the hard work they were doing and the entertainment they were providing, so two ladies set about organising a presentation to the two impresarios. It was made by the Mayor on Monday, 8 March 1934, the first anniversary of *Pygmalion*, the play that had set them on the road to success.

With their reputation growing throughout London's theatrical establishment, Fraser pressed managements to let him have production rights to West End successes as quickly as possible. In 1934 the Connaught was able to advertise 'first repertory production' on ten occasions - twice while the originals were still running on Shaftesbury Avenue. One of the two, *Ten Minute Alibi*, was seen by over 6,000 at the Connaught. Many were turned away at every performance, one of the unfortunates being James Agate who made the story the leading item in his *Sunday Times* article that week - the management did find him a seat for a later performance.

Fraser's greatest coup that year, though, was the first repertory production of *Sweet Nell of Old Drury*. This was the first play which Julia Neilson and Fred Terry had staged under their own management in 1900. For thirty years it was in their repertoire and was constantly toured in tandem with *Henry of Navarre*. After Fred Terry's death in April, 1933, Fraser wrote to Julia Neilson requesting permission to stage the play at the Connaught. This was declined, partly because it was very much Neilson's own role and partly because, although it had made her a rich and famous actress, she had always been aware that it was a load of romantic old tosh which she did not think would appeal to a repertory audience. In the following March Julia's daughter, Phyllis Neilson-Terry, revived the play in London to moderate success. Fraser applied to Julia again. This time permission was granted subject to her long-standing friend and former company general manager, Arthur Garrett, coming to Worthing to oversee the production. Julia also lent some very valuable props for the production.

It was a mammoth piece of work with eighteen principal roles and four big sets. Far from it not appealing to a repertory audience, all seats for the Saturday evening performance were sold within hours of the box office opening. Julia Neilson's health prevented her coming to Worthing but her daughter did get to the Wednesday matinee and was so impressed with the overall standard that she immediately offered to appear as a 'guest artiste' with the company if a suitable date could be found. She subsequently starred there in two of her greatest successes, *Elizabeth of England* and *Mary Tudor*.

Several other very well known-stars of the day made guest appearances with the company, including Madge Compton, Barbara Everest and the master of melodrama, Tod Slaughter, who played in *Maria Marten*.

When Raymond Lovell came to Worthing to repeat the role of Henry VIII which he created in the London production of *The Queen who Kept Her Head,* he found it remarkable that after only four days of rehearsal the company had reached the same standard it had taken the London cast four weeks to achieve. The original company had, of course, worked on a virgin script but the point was made: four

Raymond Lovell, who had created the role of Henry VIII *in the West End, came to Worthing in 1934 as a guest star in* The Queen Who Kept Her Head. *Megan Latimer, as Katherine Parr, is seen with Virginia Field. On the far right is Bill Fraser, who also directed the production. The set was by Dan Barker*

days was an incredibly short time to get to such a high standard, especially since they were performing another play at the same time. Raymond Lovell knew all about repertory standards, having run his own companies in Bournemouth and Southampton before making his name in the West End. But if Worthing was doing well it was the exception; the financial crisis, the talkies and a very hot summer had hit repertory theatre. Plymouth was on the point of closing after twenty years, Leeds, Hull and Harrogate were struggling whilst Birmingham was in such deep trouble that Barry Jackson had handed it over to a trust and it was now virtually owned by the local council. The touring circuit, too, was in dire straits. Not only were audiences dwindling but there were insufficient shows on the road to keep most theatres open all year round - some went 'dark' for weeks at a time. The Theatre Royal in Brighton decided to emulate its Worthing neighbour and turned to repertory as did theatres in York and Perth. Many theatres succumbed totally and became cinemas. In Worthing the opposite happened.

With the Plaza and Odeon cinemas open - and rumours, unfounded as it transpired, of two more to come in Worthing - it was a battle between them to get the first run of newly released films. The Rivoli was getting its fair share of popular attractions and Seebold was happy to let the Dome become the home to second runs of successful movies. The Picturedrome was his problem child.

Fraser was battling to get large casts and big sets on his pocket-handkerchief stage. Bell was frustrated at having to turn so many people away when, next door, was a cinema twice the size, with an unused stage, showing films to a handful of spectators.

The answer was obvious to all three of them.

Discussions between them were amicable but there were differences of opinion. Seebold took the view that following his alterations two years earlier the Worthing Repertory Company could move straight into the cinema. Bell, however, insisted that the entrance to the Picturedrome, a long narrow passage, would not suit theatre audiences who wanted a foyer where they could drink coffee and chat during the intervals. Seebold had reservations about this but conceded that a licensed bar would be essential. Fraser was not too happy with the stage for, although it was larger than the existing space, it was wide and shallow, all right for a line of dancing girls but not ideal for an intimate love scene.

A. T. Goldsmith, the local architect who had designed the earlier alterations, was called back to advise on essential changes. It was, he said, impossible to alter the stage but he designed a spacious new entrance with a bar above. Budgets were agreed and a new lease signed.

On 6 June 1935 the Picturedrome closed once again.

Even if the days of the small theatre were numbered, this did not prevent the presentation of large and lavish productions. The 'first repertory production' tag was up for *Richard of Bordeaux* with its 29 characters and 12 scenes. Since Bill Fraser was taking the long title role (created in London by John Gielgud) a guest director was called in, the 27-year-old Robert Morley, who had played the role of Gloucester on tour, a part he repeated in Worthing. Six weeks later, to celebrate the jubilee of King George V, another 'first' was notched up with *Clive of India* despite 37 characters and 8 sets.

The final production in the old Connaught was an aptly titled comedy by Ian Hay, *The Happy Ending.* Every seat was booked far in advance for the last performance on Saturday, 28 September 1935, and there were more than a few tears as the final curtain fell.

Large and more comfortable the new house might be, but many of the cast and audience had become attached to the cramped little Connaught.

Forty-eight hours later, as the curtain rose on the first production at the New Connaught Theatre, Worthing hit the headlines of the national press and a myth was born.

CHAPTER THREE

Fraser knew that the move to a renovated cinema was a good story, but he had neither the time nor the expertise to exploit it. He called in one of London's most successful theatre press representatives, David Brown.

Brown came to Worthing and after chatting to the partners for a couple of hours he had a story - a story vastly different from what either of them had expected. The move to the new theatre was to be the peg for a display of truly dramatic histrionics. There was nothing particularly newsworthy in having turned the corner within six months, he told them, and the money borrowed from the Fraser's parents was irrelevant. In Brown's version Bell and Fraser had pooled their meagre savings and struggled for two years, losing money every week, before recognition came. The story was embellished by the totally untrue suggestions that nobody would display posters, that tradesmen would not hire them furniture or stage properties and that people would not even accept free tickets to see the plays.

Both the partners roared with laughter: how could anyone believe a story like that? Editors would realise at once that unless they had massive resources nobody could run a theatre at a loss for two years. The press, Brown assured them, would believe anything if it made a good story and so would their readers.

On the morning of the new theatre's opening the national press wallowed in this 'rags to riches' story. Hardly a paper missed it and the headlines in the *Daily Express* were typical:

FOUR YEARS AGO TWO MEN LAID CARPETS

IN A TINY HALL....

TODAY THEY LEASE A £60,000 THEATRE

It was not until later in the week that the two men were able to relish the highly coloured publicity, which was believed not only at the time but is still trotted out, even today.

Although he had directed *The Happy Ending,* Fraser did not appear in it, knowing that his energies would be needed in preparing the new theatre. Nevertheless he had a leading role in the opening production which had to be rehearsed.

The move from one building to the other was not smooth: neither Bell, Fraser, the back stage nor front-of-house staff had much rest in the week before opening night. If not everything had been completed by the time the doors opened, even if the play itself had not had a dress rehearsal, the public was not aware of anything that had been overlooked.

Over 6,000 applications had been received for first night tickets but only 920 people were able to make their way under the smart new canopy with the theatre's name picked out in bright neon lighting. The exterior of the newly built foyer was in black and cream tiling whilst inside the decor was in cream and green art deco. The foyer was lit from four sunken panels set in the ceiling. A wide staircase led

The New Connaught Theatre

to the first floor bar, then one of the largest theatre bars in England, the curved servery running the length of the room.

The auditorium was on one level which was gently raked allowing an unrestricted view of the stage from all of the 900 seats. At the rear were four boxes seating a further twenty. The colour scheme throughout was black and green.

As soon as the doors opened a nine-piece orchestra struck up in the pit, playing for half an hour before all performances as well as during the intervals.

When the gala night audience, immaculately turned out in dinner jackets and new evening gowns, had taken its seats, Bell led on to the stage the town's Mayor, Cllr G. B. Bennett, who was one of the theatre's regular supporters. In his speech he predicted that 'the opening of this theatre in Worthing is going to have repercussions all over the country... if Fraser and Bell continue to give us the splendid performances that they have given us in the past they can rest assured of the great success of the new theatre.' The opening production was appropriately entitled *Theatre Royal.*

Few repertories had tackled Edna Furber and George Kaufman's comedy since although it had only one set it was a highly complicated one, showing several rooms in one house. As the curtain went up there was a crescendo of applause for Bert Venimore's effective design, whose main feature was a sweeping staircase.

The *Worthing Herald* recorded: 'It is the story of a theatrical family and when the curtain rose at the initial performance of the play on Monday night, a crowded audience gave it an enthusiastic reception.

'Such enthusiasm was not born merely from the play itself but from the realisation that the Connaught Rep had proved itself a band of gallant troupers and a happy 'family' and they were now reaping a reward for earnest endeavour carried to success in the face of great obstacles.

'Every permanent member of the company received a roar of applause from the Connaught 'regulars' as they appeared on the stage, the action of the play frequently held up for an appreciable period while the applause continued.'

All Worthing's favourite players were in the cast of eighteen - many of them later to become known throughout the country. Alongside Bill Fraser were Marian

Spencer, Dorothy Primrose, Jane Comfort, Raymond Francis and Gay Brune. A special round of applause went to Arthur Challoner, who was not only a regular player with the company but also its stage manager.

The auditorium which seated 920 people

The show was a good comedy with plenty of laughs, which kept the audience delighted throughout its three acts: the timing was perfect and nothing even hinted at the lack of a dress rehearsal - at the final curtain there was a standing ovation. As the cast took their calls, to their surprise a giant goodluck horseshoe was wheeled on by a group of regular playgoers. The horseshoe was laden with gifts for the cast and everyone employed in the theatre - another presentation subscribed to by grateful patrons.

One of the largest bars in the country

Everybody, the company, the staff and the audience toasted the new venture in champagne. 'It is the biggest moment in our lives,' Bill Fraser told them, 'the great tragedy is that we are so tired and have been so busy that we can't really appreciate a good night like this.'

Fraser and Bell were not the only ones who were tired: when Joe Danton, the theatre's carpenter, took his seat to watch the show he fell sound asleep and missed all the first act!

Everybody in the town wanted to see inside the new theatre and, once again, the week was a complete sell out.

While everything was fine in front of the footlights, it was not quite so perfect behind the scenes. Fraser had been right, the stage was too wide and shallow. The garage they had used for painting the sets was no longer large enough to handle the size of scenery that was needed for the new stage: the backcloths now had to be painted on a frame attached to the back wall of the theatre, reducing the depth of the stage still further. For some productions, actors making their entrances from the opposite side to their dressing rooms had to creep under the stage to get there. The acoustics, too, were such that the actors had to face 'out front' as much as possible instead of facing each other when playing a scene. Somehow, over the years successive generations of actors have managed to make this appear almost natural.

Despite the technical problems, the policy remained the same: weekly changes of plays soundly acted and well staged. Not all the productions commanded full houses: their sixth show in the new theatre was a lavish presentation of Andre

Obey's drama, *Noah*, but the idea of seeing their favourite actors disguised by animal skins did not appeal to Worthing audiences and they stayed away. But this was an exception and, like the 'first repertory production' sticker, the 'House Full' boards were outside the theatre more often than not. There was, too, an increasing number of visits from well-known guest players.

Authors often came to see Worthing productions of their plays. When Norman Ginsbury saw the first night of his *Viceroy Sarah* he was so impressed that he returned later in the week bringing a large party of friends. During the interval he congratulated Bell on having 'the best repertory company in the country'.

Mention and praise in the national press became almost commonplace. George Bishop, writing in *The Sunday Times*, was typical:

'I spent an evening recently at the New Connaught Theatre at Worthing.... It was an interesting experience. The theatre is a handsome building, attractively decorated and finely equipped. The night I was there it was packed and at the end of the performance between 200 and 300 cars drove up to take the audience away. During the intervals the foyer and the big horseshoe-shaped bar were crowded and one had the impression of a club in which the same people met each other week after week.

'Theatre-going in Worthing is now an established institution, a definite habit. Perhaps the most remarkable thing is that the audiences vary little. On Saturday nights, I was told, there are usually only 50 casual playgoers in the house.'

Another writer, Richard Clowes, again in *The Sunday Times,* described how supporters were coming regularly from as far afield as Eastbourne, Portsmouth and Horsham.

Whereas before Bell and Fraser arrived in the town, Worthing residents had travelled to Brighton for their entertainment, by 1937 the reverse was true. The reasons, according to the *Brighton and Hove Herald* were:

'There is a constant complaint that the presentation of plays at the Theatre Royal is not good enough. A typical utterance is "I am not going to see those amateurs...". "You must get the stars," say the critics, "the rest will follow." The best reply to this criticism is to be found at the New Connaught Theatre, Worthing.

'The plays and performances at Worthing are perhaps a little better all round than at Brighton of late. But the difference in these matters is not sufficient to account for the fact that the Worthing theatre succeeds financially while the Brighton theatre fails financially. One finds as a fact that a number of theatre lovers have deserted the Brighton theatre and go regularly once a week to the Worthing theatre despite the extra cost in time and money. Why is this? The answer given, by some at least, is that the organisation of the Worthing theatre is better. Its social qualities are more appealing. A gathering at the Worthing theatre is a gathering of old friends welcomed by all at the theatre as such.'

The Connaught was recognised as one of the leaders among the twenty full-time repertories in the country. When, in 1937, the prestigious monthly pictorial magazine *Theatre World* commissioned George Fearon to contribute a series of articles on British repertories the very first featured was Worthing.

Despite their success and hard work, local relations remained of paramount importance to Fraser. Late in 1937 a Save the Downland Fund was set up. Particularly interested in this was Nancy Price, a Worthing resident and leading West End actress, then appearing at the Playhouse in the phenomenally successful play *Whiteoaks*.

Fraser and Bell suggested that she and the London company should do a Monday matinee at the Connaught with every penny of the takings going to the Fund. A replica of the London set was built by the Connaught and members of the company acted as ushers and programme sellers. The Duke of Norfolk was amongst the full house, which raised over £1,000. The cost to Bell and Fraser of opening their current production on Tuesday instead of the usual Monday was reckoned to be at least £100. (In a smaller way, over fifty years later, Carol Hodges remembered how when the Worthing Central Townswomen's Guild won their heat of a drama festival, Fraser gave them three sessions of coaching before they went into the County finals.)

During 1938 the Connaught suffered, like all entertainments, from the Munich crisis. For several weeks before Neville Chamberlain returned from his meeting with Hitler promising 'peace in our time', audiences had been staying at home to listen to the latest news on the radio. During the crisis Bell and Fraser enrolled as Air Raid Wardens.

That October, to celebrate the sixth anniversary of Fraser and Bell's arrival in the town, the general run of popular successes was broken for a week by a production of *Hamlet,* the first Shakespeare at either Connaught since the departure of the Bragg-Liddell company in 1932.

Although Grey Blake, who played the title role, was not in the previous week's production, the rest of the principal players had been. In spite of only four days' rehearsal, this big production was a huge success with both the large audiences and the local press. Ophelia was played by Dorothy Primrose, who had been with the company on and off for four years: later she repeated the role with great distinction opposite Alec Clunes, both at London's Arts Theatre and on a highly prestigious post-war tour of Europe. An oil painting of her in the role at Worthing by S. M. Weins is now in the collection of the Worthing Museum and Art Gallery. As well as directing, Bill Fraser played the Grave Digger - after the performance he admitted he had never been so nervous of a production since their very first at the old theatre.

Six weeks later the company revived Shaw's *St. Joan* (with better speaking and a larger cast, this time).

It was hardly surprising that the strain of continually planning, directing, casting and acting was beginning to tell on Fraser, who had also found time to do several broadcasts and appear in his first film, *Murder in the Family*. Early in 1939 he was taken ill and three months away from the Connaught was ordered. Charles Bell continued to manage the company and Reginald Brooke, who had appeared in one or two productions at the old theatre, took over as director.

The problems Fraser faced on his return were those confronting everyone: the deteriorating political situation in Europe and the increasing likelihood of war. Business was still good, however, and a major coup had been to persuade one of the best loved veterans of the day, Sir Seymour Hicks, to appear for a week. He played to excellent business in *The Last Trump* by James Bridie at the beginning of August and another 'big name' had been booked for the first week of September.

The run of *Whiteoaks* at the Playhouse had come to an end and Nancy Price had agreed to join her 'local repertory' to repeat the role of Gran which she had already played over 1,300 times. Packed houses were expected for the production which was scheduled for the week of 4 September 1939.

War was declared that Sunday morning.

Fearing the massive air-raids that had been the hallmark of Nazi Germany's annexing moves in Europe, all places of entertainment were immediately closed on government orders. In the absence of the anticipated devastation, however, the ban was lifted after a few days and *Whiteoaks* opened the following week on 11 September, the curtain now going up an hour earlier at 7.00pm since the latest government orders decreed that all places of entertainment must be closed by 10.00pm.

The outbreak of war brought masses of Londoners to nearby Brighton and as West End shows deserted the capital to go on tour, the town's Theatre Royal played to packed houses that autumn; but in Worthing it was a very different story. Holidaymakers had left town, most residents were not in the mood to venture out in the rigidly imposed blackout and regular supporters from outlying districts were not going to drive to Worthing at night.

Frank Petley, a popular member of Bill Fraser's company

Although business slumped, the Connaught kept going with some light-hearted fare and just a month after war was declared Fraser was asked to mount a tour round the troops stationed in the south of England: Worthing had achieved another 'first', the first repertory company to be engaged by ENSA, the central organisation set up to provide entertainment for the forces. Two plays, *Nothing but the Truth* and *It's a Boy* set off along the south coast on 8 October, touring for three weeks.

After the pantomime a variety show was staged at the Connaught. 'We are not changing our policy to variety,' Bell told the press, 'but this experiment should act as a feeler - if Worthing wants a variety bill now and again they can have it. We are out to cater for all tastes.' Two popular radio acts, Norman Long and Leslie Strange, headed the bill while Fraser and the company appeared in a sketch. They played twice-nightly with two matinees but business was still not good.

To add to the problems the war was causing, it was a very severe winter.

By the beginning of February the situation was becoming desperate. Around fifty people were employed at the theatre and the only income was through the box office; the loss - which was growing every week - was down to Bell and Fraser. Although they had done well for five years, with the move to the larger theatre their overheads had increased enormously. What they had managed to save was being whittled away and in the international situation there was no way they would borrow again.

Interviewed by the local press they admitted that keeping the theatre open since the war had imposed a considerable strain on both of them, a strain they did not feel justified in continuing unless the public showed some sign of increasing its support.

'The time has come,' said Bell, 'when we must appeal to the Worthing public on our own behalf. We have appealed to them successfully on behalf of other good causes and now we ask them to help save the real theatre in Worthing. All we ask them to do is support us.'

Letters to the press followed: one suggested reviving *Pygmalion*, history might repeat itself and save the theatre again. The suggestion was taken up, ironically in the first week of March, the week of salvation seven years earlier, but that success was not repeated. Practical support came from the local furnishers, Jordan and Cook, who had often hired furniture to the company, which they were now prepared to do without charge.

Just as they were facing these problems, the London-based writer, Eric Maschwitz, was planning a new revue for the Comedy Theatre. Called *New Faces*, it was not going to have any recognised stars but the company would consist of 'boys and girls from the repertories'. When Bill Fraser was offered a part he could not refuse.

Leslie Handford was engaged to direct productions in Worthing while Fraser was away, but business remained bad. It picked up during the Easter weekend, when the town was packed with holidaymakers, but soon after this France was invaded by Germany.

An attack on Britain seemed inevitable. The south coast was becoming the front line. There was yet another problem: with young actors liable to be called on to report for military service at forty-eight hours notice or less, casting juvenile leads became almost impossible.

Bell decided he could carry on no longer and announced that the theatre would close on 15 June 1940 after the final performance of *Quiet Wedding.* News came through on the eve of that performance that the Germans had captured Paris.

The closure came with a little sadness and a great deal of relief: long standing patrons were sorry to see the end of the venture but company members just wanted to get away from the coast and be with their families. Many years later, Pamela Parkin, who had played a leading role in that last show, recalled that it was a beautiful hot June evening but as she went to the stage door to get a breath of air during the interval she found 'you could almost smell fear everywhere.'

Just five weeks after his critically applauded London debut, Bill Fraser's own farewell at the theatre was in a Sunday evening charity concert organised by Bud Flanagan and the Crazy Gang, all local residents. Despite a bill which included such legendary characters as Max Miller, Will Fyffe, Billy Cotton, Charlie Kunz, Evelyn Laye and all six members of the Crazy Gang, Fraser was given the 'star' spot in the show. His next appearance on stage in the town was to be as lead comedian in the 1951 summer show at the Pier Pavilion.

Since their opening night in October 1932, Bell and Fraser had been responsible for 365 productions at the two theatres, of which 192 were first repertory productions. They had staged 8 plays by Shaw, 6 by John Galsworthy, 7 of Priestley's and had launched five new plays, two of which had found their way into the West End.

The success did not rest just with Charles Bell and Bill Fraser, however. During their seven years in the town not only had they built up a loyal audience but also many of the cast became entrenched in Worthing.

In the nineteen-thirties many who worked in weekly repertory were expected to become proficient at almost everything. Arthur Challoner, who stayed six years, was originally engaged as stage manager but before long he was also on stage, sometimes in leading roles; he directed productions on the odd occasion when Fraser wanted a week off and when special lighting effects were required in a show it was Challoner who was called on to design them.

Fraser and Bell worked hard but they enjoyed life, that enjoyment manifesting itself in regular after-the-show parties when substantial amounts of scotch were consumed. Unlike West End and touring productions, where the stars remained aloof, there was no hierarchy in the Worthing company: everyone was treated alike.

Peter Cushing, in his autobiography, related how his first meeting with Fraser, which resulted in his making his stage debut in a walk-on part, ended in a hectic binge.

It was this camaraderie that appealed to Frank Petley, a deeply religious man with a fund of the bluest imaginable stories. He was well-known in London and on Broadway as a 'second lead' player, rarely the star but invariably the principal supporting actor. He was also one of the first of the theatrical community to make his home in Brighton. Fraser had invited him to 'guest' in the important role of the Archbishop in the 1933 production of *St. Joan*. At the end of the week Petley, who was then 61, suggested to Fraser that he should become a member of the company, taking time off from Worthing if any worthwhile West End roles came up - which they regularly did. When war closed the Connaught he was immediately snapped up by the Old Vic for the roles of Othello and Falstaff in *The Merry Wives of Windsor*.

He and another experienced actor, F. Payne Palmer, known to everybody as 'Uncle', formed a strong backbone to the company and were happy to pass on their knowledge and experience to newcomers. Among these, Nigel Patrick, Leslie Phillips and Desmond Walter-Ellis became household names. Two popular young actors whose careers began in Worthing became very influential in other spheres of theatre: Stephen Arlen took control, first of the Old Vic and subsequently of the English National Opera, while Douglas Searle became one of the most notable of the post-war directors of the Birmingham repertory, later going to America as a foremost director of opera and drama.

Life was not quite so settled for the ladies in the company. Fraser believed, rightly or wrongly, that although an actor could play a multitude of different parts without disappointing the audience, after a few months the average playgoer would tire of even the most accomplished actress. Many distinguished actresses spent the early days of their career in Worthing, most doing their few months, then moving elsewhere for a while before returning to the Connaught for another spell.

Among the young actresses who went far was Marian Spencer, who played the leads in many West End productions, often opposite Ralph Richardson or John Gielgud. Virginia Field left Worthing in 1934 to make her first film and within three years she had graduated to a very successful career in Hollywood. Dorothy Primrose, who was eighteen when she first joined the company, was still appearing regularly at the Connaught five years later and, like Raymond Francis, who stayed for three years, returned to Worthing many more times under different managements.

Although television was in its infancy before the war, BBC radio had established a highly regarded drama repertory company which recruited three of its most popular and versatile voices from Worthing in Gladys Spencer, Richard Hurndall and Lewis Stringer.

Throughout their stay Fraser was the main director and although there were reliefs, none of his stand-ins achieved any future reputation in this field.

Many repertory players of that time had no ambition for fame and fortune. They enjoyed the corporate life that a repertory provided - some, if they got a part in a London show or in a touring production, found that with nothing to do until performance time, the day dragged and they couldn't wait to get back to rep. Life in Worthing was hard but fun and for anyone with experience Bell and Fraser were not mean employers: the average wage had risen to £4 for girls, £6 for the men and up to £10 for a leading player.

Fraser's start on the ladder of fame came with his debut in *New Faces*. After war service as a signals officer in the RAF he concentrated on light entertainment, both in London and in seaside summer shows, several of which he staged himself. His home base remained in Worthing until the death of his mother in 1957 which coincided with his television 'break' in *The Army Game*. Interviewed for *Radio Times* in 1974, he looked back on his Connaught days. 'It was a hard time,' he said, 'but probably the hapiest of my life. I was young, ambitious, brim full of determination and it seemed that everything I wanted was there. I didn't want to be a big star, I never wanted that. I just wanted to have my own theatre, my own company. The war closed it down and I never got it back.'

Right up until his death in 1987 he kept a fatherly eye on the Connaught. His only other appearance on its stage was at a Sunday evening show in 1968 but he was among the audience on 30 September 1985, the fiftieth-anniversary celebration of the opening of the New Connaught Theatre.

Fate was not so kind to Charles Bell. At the closure of the Connaught he moved to nearby Steyning to look after a friend's farm; but he was a man of the theatre, not of the land. He then joined ENSA and was appointed to run the Devonshire Park Theatre in Eastbourne as a Garrison Theatre for troops stationed in the area. At the end of the war, with the help of a loan from Fraser, he took a lease on the Eastbourne theatre, bringing in a succession of touring shows. At first this policy paid off handsomely and at the end of twelve months he had paid off his debt and added 10% interest, but then the fortunes of the Devonshire Park declined. Repertory was tried and failed. In 1952 Bell was declared bankrupt, owing more than £5,000. Denying the Official Receiver's allegations of living an extravagant life style, he did admit to having neglected the business and frequently being away from the theatre for days at a time. Thus did Bell's involvement in the entertainment industry come to an end.

The demise of the Worthing Repertory Company was just another casualty of the war. Luckily it was one that would be reborn just as successfully at a later date.

CHAPTER FOUR

Seaside towns were deserted. There were no holiday visitors, children were being evacuated to America and Canada, many of the elderly left for country areas; only those who had to, those who refused to budge and the servicemen stationed roundabout stayed at the coast.

Everyone was doing his bit to help defend the country. The men who had not been called up spent their evening as Air Raid Wardens or learned to shoulder pikes and pick-axe handles in the Home Guard. Women played their part in the Women's Voluntary Services, air raid precautions, learned first aid and took over many men's jobs.

In June 1940, Worthing's three largest hotels closed.

The hot, uneasy summer was passing slowly. Air raids began in earnest, at first in daylight then, in October, the night onslaught on London began. It was not a time for going out to the theatre: the radio was the main source of amusement. Tommy Handley's *It's That Man Again* did much to keep up the country's morale and its many catch-phrases became part of the language of the day.

Humour was homespun but towards the end of 1940 the nation had come to terms with its fears and there was a general feeling of live for the day, make the best of it.

Since the repertory company had moved into the new theatre, the old Connaught Hall had remained unused - a plan to turn it into a news cinema had been turned down by the council. That November Worthing's Home Guard decided to put on a revue for a few nights and Seebold was happy to let them have the hall and re-christen it the Garrison Theatre.

There was a good deal of talent amongst the Home Guard and their acquaintances, an ex-*Fol-de-Rols* comedian, a former member of the Sheffield rep, a Tiller Girl or two, plus Cyril Campion, a rising author of plays and revue sketches. Stanley Holt was a composer and Daniel Barker, Fraser's first designer, did the sets. There were sufficient musicians to form a band whose leader was the appropriately named Sergeant J. Sussex.

The show was a success, audiences included not only other members of the Home Guard but servicemen and local residents. With several changes of programme, Worthing's Garrison Theatre was filled for five weeks. They decided to embark on a Christmas pantomime and as Cyril Campion set to work on the script for *Red Riding Hood* the plans were announced in the local press.

Out of the blue a company calling itself South Coast Productions proposed reopening the New Connaught Theatre as a variety house. What better than to raise the curtain with a pantomime? Negotiations were rapidly completed and on Boxing Day, instead of being in the old hall, *Red Riding Hood* was at the far better equipped theatre next door.

South Coast Productions announced that their variety shows would be staged twice daily with matinee and evening performances, and on Sundays there were to be concerts. The venture really got under way on Monday, 13 January, with a revue which, since it was now 1941, was rather ineptly named *Naughty Girls of 1940.*

Within a week the theatre was closed again.

During 1941 tension began to ease and, like other south coast towns, Worthing became a military training ground for masses of British and Allied servicemen. That autumn travel became more difficult, buses packed up early and were town-based, trains were unreliable, crowded and cold: unless it was for business, nobody wanted to travel to London and even a trip to Brighton was not easy. Entertainment had to be found locally.

Liquor supplies to public houses were in short supply and they were often forced to restrict their opening hours. The cinemas were doing a roaring trade, everybody was looking for amusement.

Seebold knew that Connaught had to reopen but since, as ten years earlier, there were insufficient new movies going round to supply five venues, it would have to be as a theatre.

That October he joined forces with George Stevens, a former manager of the local Odeon cinema, to get the Connaught going again. The policy was to provide the best live entertainment available. Stevens, when the plans were made public, declared, 'I am convinced that there is a real need in Worthing for a theatre which sets out to cater for the town's special requirements - it is no good offering Worthing anything second rate.' His experiences at the Odeon, he felt sure, had given him a shrewd idea of what the town would accept.

The opening night augured well for the future. The Connaught Theatre (the word 'New' was now dropped from the name) was full for *Flying Colours*, a musical spectacular which had just finished a very successful run at London's Phoenix Theatre. This was followed by the premiere of Kenneth Horne's comedy, *Love in a Mist,* with a cast starring Ann Todd, Richard Bird, Michael Shepley and Marjorie Reynolds, four very big names.

It seemed that Worthing really was to have top class entertainment. Among those who appeared at the Connaught in the early days of the new management were 'star' names such as Jack Hulbert and Cicely Courtneidge, Frank Forbes Robertson, Victoria Hopper, Tom Walls, Betty Marsden and Mary Morris. All of these played to good houses but there were dull weeks when attractions were routine rather than first class and the box office returns were appalling.

By the middle of February, only sixteen weeks after the grand reopening night, the supply of good touring shows had completely dried up. On the billboards appeared such titles as *Flashes from the B.B.C., Blue Pencil* and *H.M.S. Laughter.*

Within a week or two of the decline, George Stevens left and Seebold took control of the bookings. His first move was to bring in the well-known Court Players for a repertory season. His reasoning was simple: the Bell-Fraser company had built up a tremendous following for repertory and the past few weeks had shown that there was no loyal support for a succession of different companies of varying standards. He wanted steady returns, not one good week followed by three bad ones.

Harry Hanson had successfully run several companies under the name of the Court Players who did long or short seasons throughout the country. They had built up a reputation for competent productions of middle of the road, popular successes. Harry Bristow, manager of the company which came to Worthing, summed up the policy when he said: 'of one thing I am sure: that is Worthing won't stand for suggestive stuff. Good clean wholesome plays are what they want, good clean wholesome plays are what we are going to give them.'

Under a bold headline 'Court Repertory has Come To Stay', the *Worthing Herald* reported Bristow as saying it was hoped to stay here indefinitely.

'We believe Worthing will support us loyally.' He went on to tell the reporter of the eagerness with which the public was welcoming repertory back to Worthing again. 'They'll need no winning over for the Court Players have a brilliant reputation and Worthing has always had a soft spot for repertory.' Brave and confident words!

Rebecca was the opening choice but it appeared that this was not the sort of good, clean, wholesome play to attract Worthing audiences. Comedy, drama, farce and thrillers followed, but audiences stayed away. Under the pseudonym 'Old Stager' a letter appeared in the *Worthing Herald* extolling the merits of the Court Players, declaring them every bit as talented as the Bell-Fraser crowd. The letter ended with a plea: 'Surely it is up to the Worthing theatre-lovers to support this brave endeavour to keep the live stage going and to attend in sufficient force to make the enterprise pay. Go to it, Worthing folks!'

In fact, after six or seven weeks audiences did begin to pick up but it was too late: the Court Players announced that they were packing their bags on 13 June, but for once the Connaught did not close. Hastily Seebold arranged a summer show and during its run he was in touch with Hanson again. He was convinced that the Court Players hadn't given Worthing a long enough trial and Hanson was persuaded to try another of his companies for an eight week season opening on 10 August.

The diet was the same as before but it seemed that Seebold had been right in trying again. The first night of A.J. Cronin's *Jupiter Laughs* was seen by a large and enthusiastic audience and so it continued throughout the eight weeks. For October, Seebold had already engaged the Clarkson Rose-Olive Fox *Twinkle* revue company, a sure-fire success for any coastal and many an inland town. There was no difficulty in persuading Harry Hanson's company to make a third visit after *Twinkle.*

The *Worthing Herald* noted in a leader that 'recent visits from *Twinkle* and different companies of Harry Hanson's Court Players have lifted the Worthing theatre back from the slough of despond into which it had fallen, to its proper place in the town's social life.'

The Court Players returned on 2 November with the popular thriller, *Ladies in Retirement.* The following Sunday afternoon the outstanding Irish tenor, John McCormack, gave a recital accompanied by Gerald Moore and a young violinist, Harold Fielding (who, a few years later, was to become closely associated with the Connaught).

With a two-week break for the Christmas pantomime, the third season of the Court Players lasted thirty-two weeks. Weeks of good clean, wholesome plays which Worthing did like, despite the fact that from the beginning of 1943 the last bus out of the town centre left at 9.00p.m. so that performances had to begin at 6.30.

Life in a repertory company during the war was not easy. Margery Mason recalled her time in Worthing: 'Certainly attempts were made to set the plays well and there was a standard of competence, if nothing more, among the players. Actors were in short supply, being either too old, too young or medically unfit for active service. We were lucky in having a conscientious objector in his early thirties.

'Clothes were on ration but Harry Hanson stuck to his rules for his actresses: never wear black in a comedy, no two actresses in the same colour and don't repeat a dress within six weeks. This was partly overcome by borrowing within the Hanson network: the call would go out to Hastings or Leeds or wherever, "Lend me the blue negligee this week and you can have the red suit whenever you need it."

'Fans donated evening gowns which they despaired of ever wearing again and there was a second-hand shop nearby where you could pick up threadbare bits and pieces for a few pence.

'But there was the consolation that Worthing was quite a nice place to be at. Quiet, reasonably safe and there was the sea beyond the barbed wire.'

From the management's point of view, life was not made any easier when the Entertainments Tax went up to one-third of the gross takings; like most theatres, the Connaught absorbed the increase and left seat prices unaltered.

Seebold decided to give audiences a break from repertory in the summer and for three months a series of summer revues took the stage: this was the time when the nation was being asked to spend its holidays at home.

Strangely, the Court Players declined an invitation to return to the Connaught that autumn and Seebold cast around for another repertory. His choice fell on a relatively new company, the Fortune Players under the direction of Barbara Borrow who, with her husband, had been running the Castle Theatre at Farnham. They were to play from early October until Christmas and return for the winter of 1944.

Seebold had a fortnight to fill between the summer shows and the new repertory season. He did it with two touring productions, one of which was Noel Coward's *Blithe Spirit*. Still playing to packed houses in London, several tours were sent out and this was the first time the play had come to Worthing. There were no well-known names in the cast - the play itself was the draw - yet it was the Connaught's biggest box office success since the outbreak of the war.

The Fortune Players opened with another recent London success, *Murder Without Crime* but once again Worthing did not want to know a new company. Looking around for young actors, the company was pleased to be approached by a young lad who wanted to go on the stage. Untrained and with no experience, Reginald Marsh made his debut in the company's third production, *Eden End*. Playing opposite him was John Witty, then serving with the RAF but earning some pin money whilst on fourteen days' leave. 'I was a very raw young actor who had no idea what acting was all about and was terrified that I wouldn't know the lines, never having had to learn so much in such a short time,' Marsh remembered. 'John helped me and really gave me the only lessons in acting that I ever received.'

Plays by Priestley, John Van Druten, Emlyn Williams and Terence Rattigan all failed. It began to look as though Worthing was opposed to change: if their favourites, the Court Players, were not coming back they didn't want to risk their money on something they didn't know. Nothing had changed, it seemed, since the days of Gwladys Wheeler.

Bad though business was, the last straw came for the Fortune Players when takings were mysteriously 'borrowed' from the box office. The company did not return to the Connaught after the pantomime.

1944 opened to another hiatus. In the absence of a repertory company, Seebold found himself forced to bring back touring shows and a ropey old lot they were - he was beginning bitterly to regret having gone back into live entertainment. Luckily the profits from his two cinemas were comfortably able to subsidise the Connaught.

The only bright spot that spring was Worthing's first visit from a ballet company for many years, when Lydia Kyasht's Russian Ballet appeared for a profitable week.

The situation was becoming desperate. What could be done? It seemed that Worthing was only prepared to support repertory and then only after the company had had time to dig itself in. Few companies were prepared to play to empty houses for eight to ten weeks in the hope that support would eventually build up when the word got around.

The only answer seemed to be for the management to form its own company. So it was that on 3 April 1944 the Hexagon Players, formed by Percy Busby, manager of the theatre, made their first appearance. Again the policy was high class productions, this time with real West End artists. Dennis Bowen, who had just completed a run at the Comedy Theatre, was the leading man and the resident director was Sybil Wise who had been a popular member of the Bell-Fraser company for a while.

The *Worthing Herald* declared that the Hexagon Players was a theatrical enterprise with players of quality which Worthing must support. For a change there were good houses at first. Within the first fortnight, however, came the first setback: the departure of Dennis Bowen for another West End role. The good support vanished with his departure and a revival of *Pygmalion* played to poor houses. The premiere of a new play by Michael Egan, author of the long-running *Dominant Sex*, did little to improve the situation but this time Seebold was not too concerned at the declining business.

Just as the Hexagon Players took to the stage he had received an approach from by a company which wanted to take a lease on the Connaught. Although the company was fairly new, its directors were experienced theatre people and it enjoyed financial backing from one of the biggest names in Britain's entertainment business. Seebold was only too eager to get the theatre off his hands again. As usual with him, negotiations were rapidly completed and after only eight weeks the Hexagon Players were disbanded.

The final show was Lillian Hellman's gripping war drama, *Watch on the Rhine*, and, once more, it was the final production that was best supported. The theatre then closed for two weeks to prepare for the arrival of the Overture Players. How long, people asked, would they last?

CHAPTER FIVE

The new company opened on 12 June 1944, a week after the Allied Forces had launched their invasion of Europe. There was an air of optimism everywhere.

Although London was enduring flying bombs the theatre was about to take enormous strides. Laurence Olivier, Ralph Richardson and John Burrell had been released from the Services to set up a new Old Vic Company at the New Theatre (now the Albery), while a few hundred yards away the tiny Arts Theatre Club, which Alec Clunes had been running for a couple of years, was poised to play a major part in London's theatre life.

During the war the number of provincial repertory companies had been increasing and with the arrival of the Overture Players the Connaught soon regained its position amongst the leaders.

The theatre's two-week closure enabled it to be given its first thorough spruce-up since it had opened nine years earlier. Before the first night a gala reception was held for the press and local dignitaries in the flower-decked bar. Jack Twyman, the business manager, announced the company's policy: to combine revivals of old favourites with productions of current London successes. West End directors were to be engaged and well-known film stars would join the company for short seasons. His intention was to establish a permanent repertory theatre of which the town could be proud, comments that were not new to Worthing.

Overture Theatre Ltd., the parent company, had as its directors Moie Charles and Barbara Toy, two ladies who had done everything in repertory theatres from sweeping the stage to playing leading roles, from painting the sets to writing the plays. A little later they dramatised Agatha Christie's novel *Murder at the Vicarage* in a manner which so impressed the author that she then allowed them to work on *The Hollow* - a book which she herself thought impossible to dramatise: both were highly successful. It was, however their dramatisation of another novel, Lady Eleanor Smith's *The Man in Grey,* which brought them into contact with the J. Arthur Rank Organisation.

Rank had a tremendous success with the film of *The Man in Grey,* which was the first of a series of screen costume melodramas which made stars of James Mason, Margaret Lockwood, Stewart Granger and Phyllis Calvert.

It was the film rather than the novel which Charles and Toy took as the basis for their play, knowing that, trading on the fame of the screen version, their stage adaptation would appeal to the reps. During meetings with the Rank management it became obvious that the giant film-maker was looking forward to the end of the war and the return of hundreds of would-be film actors to 'civvy street'. Few stars had been created during the war years and new talent would have to be found, and trained.

The Overture Players Company was set up with substantial financial input from Rank on the basis that the repertory company would provide a base where potential 'starlets' could find their feet in front of a live audience.

For their opening at the Connaught they staged the first repertory production of Agatha Christie's *Ten Little Niggers* (now known as *And Then There Were None*) which had run in London for almost a year and which was bound to attract local audiences. There were no 'starlets' for this production but Frank Petley made a very welcome return to Worthing in the leading role. He remained with the Overture Players until his death six months later.

If the 'House Full' boards did not come out that week, the Connaught did well enough: the takings were encouraging and the local press was enthusiastic. A leader in the *Worthing Herald* welcomed the company and hoped they would establish repertory on a firm footing in the town. The writer predicted that after the war drama would again prosper in Worthing and urged residents to support the Players.

A few weeks later the *Herald* followed this up with a lengthy article attributed to Vivien Leigh, supporting that opinion. Some readers were surprised that such a busy actress who, as everyone knew from the extensive media coverage, had just started filming *Caesar and Cleopatra*, found time to read the country's local papers, but those in the know recognised a cute publicity move by the Rank Organisation's highly professional press office.

It was with the second production that the first of many guest players appeared. Joan Greenwood, then just 23, had already made several films and her name was becoming well-known to regular cinema-goers. During a five-week stay in Worthing she played a variety of roles from the dream girl in Barrie's *Dear Brutus* to Bessie Watty in *The Corn is Green*, all of which were warmly received. With *The Corn is Green* the company first fulfilled its promise of giving leading roles to promising youngsters when eighteen-year-old Bryan Forbes took the role of Morgan Evans.

During the war years the Connaught, like many theatres, had played three matinees a week on Wednesdays, Thursdays and Saturdays. At first the Overture Players followed this pattern but instead of opening on Monday the first night became Tuesday. Audiences, however, grew fast and in response to public pressure Monday opening returned after only four weeks and the Thursday matinee was dropped.

The seventh production, Shaw's *Arms and the Man*, sold out at several performances and the following week's programme commented that the dusting off of the 'House Full' boards, which had not been seen outside the Connaught for some while, proved that the company's efforts to 'please, entertain and satisfy patrons' were bearing fruit. 'It is such a relief to be playing to live and appreciative audiences,' the programme note added.

Joyce Howard, another popular young actress, broke her rapid rise to fame in the film world to follow Joan Greenwood for five productions ranging from Shaw to Priestley via Barrie (*Quality Street* was staged only six weeks after his *Dear Brutus*), but her outstanding success was as Juliet in Shakespeare's *Romeo and Juliet.*

It was with this production that the advantages of having strong financial backing became apparent. Presented in September, it was made possible by staging a small-cast play with a guest director the previous week in order to have a full fortnight's rehearsal for the Shakespeare.

It was a distinguished production with Bryan Forbes as Mercutio and John Wynn as Romeo. Even the most optimistic of companies would have been amazed at Worthing's response to Shakespeare - an author then, more often than not, shunned by provincial audiences as incomprehensible and boring. From the opening night the theatre was packed and early in the week it was realised that there was sufficient demand to run it for another week, the first time at the new theatre that a play had run for a fortnight. The Overture Players had been accepted.

The choice of plays during the first three months was wide, with the two Barrie comedies, Shaw, Priestley's latest success, *They Came to a City,* and the

Valerie Hobson was one of Britain's most popular film stars when she appeared as a guest with the Overture Players in 1944

Shakespeare. During the weeks to Christmas the same sort of programme continued with another Shaw, an Emlyn Williams and an American political drama, *Thunder Rock*, leavened with a few recent West End successes and pre-war light comedies plus two new plays.

Although no longer joining the company for five weeks, the number of guest players increased, with appearances by Valerie Hobson, Anne Crawford, Shelagh Fraser and the return of Terence de Marney, all then at the peak of their careers. Directors during those first few months included Anthony Hawtry, who was busy establishing the Embassy Theatre at Swiss Cottage as a 'fringe' house, Peter Cresswell, a leading drama director at the B.B.C., Peter Cotes and Peter Copley.

When the season ended to make way for a far from distinguished pantomime the Overture Players had built up a large following of regulars who were eager to know what was in store for them in 1945.

1945, in fact, firmly established the Connaught as a vibrant theatre. Although Brighton was becoming an important touring date, attracting many top-class shows with big name 'stars', theatre-goers were again taking the train to Worthing for a night at the Connaught.

There was a change of policy when, in January, Peter Copley was appointed resident director - a post he held for only four months before going to the Old Vic

Charles Morgan heads towards the wicket at one of the annual Players v. Playgoers Club cricket matches at Worthing's Manor Ground

to play Edmund to Olivier's King Lear (he stayed with the Old Vic for five years).

At that time specialist directors were in the minority whether in London or in repertory and most plays were directed by actors. Like Bill Fraser, many of them were not content with directing the show but would play a leading role as well, yet neither facet appeared to suffer; Copley was among them.

Fifty-two years later, back at the Albery Theatre, where he was playing the role of Firs in the Royal Shakespeare Company's production of Chekhov's *The Cherry Orchard,* Copley - aged 82 - remembered his time in Worthing.

He was left largely to his own devices in the choice of productions and players, though occasionally a call would come through from head office in Charing Cross Road suggesting a play title. Finance never caused any problems although pressure of time occasionally did.

Twelfth Night was planned for a week in March and, being Shakespeare, two weeks of rehearsal were thought essential. He chose *There's Always Juliet,* a John Van Druten comedy which had two major characters and two much smaller supporting roles for the preceding week. Copley decided not only to direct the two plays but to play the leading male part in the Van Druten piece. Playing opposite him was Jill Barrie who had recently done the part elsewhere. Copley rehearsed *Twelfth Night* during the day and in the evenings he and Jill Barrie would find an odd corner and work on the other play - after he had appeared on stage in Chekhov's monologue, *On the Harmfulness of Tobacco,* as a curtain raiser to Shaw's *Candida.* It was lucky that *There's Always Juliet* was a straightforward piece, since there was no time for a full dress rehearsal or even a proper run-through: yet the first night went smoothly and the press reviews were enthusiastic about the performances and the direction! Looking back Copley had no idea how he had coped with getting the show on but he remembered that it was really Jill Barrie who carried the evening.

Copley felt that there was sufficient enthusiasm amongst the Connaught's regularaudience to form a playgoers' club. The inaugural meeting, on 11 February 1945, was addressed by two of the country's best-loved players, Miles Malleson and Pamela Brown (Copley's wife although at the time the marriage had become rather shaky); it was well attended and the Club soon became a lively part of the Connaught's activities, reviving the social link between town and theatre which, in a different way, Bell and Fraser had developed. Many theatre celebrities popped in on Sundays to give talks. There were regular parties, receptions for the cast, playwriting competitions and the annual cricket match between Players and Playgoers became an important fixture in Worthing's summer programme.

During his short stay, Copley continued the policy of staging a catholic range of plays: Bridie, Wilde, Priestley, Shaw, Rattigan, Shakespeare, Coward and Maugham were all represented.

When Copley left, Molly Terraine and William Sharpe shared directing duties, usually alternating productions; but still guest directors were called on - it was at Pamela Brown's suggestion that Christopher Fry directed Patrick Hamilton's famous thriller, *Rope.* Another name which appeared on the programme several times as actor or director or both was that of Guy Verney. Although not yet 30, he had carved himself a notable career as an actor on both stage and film and had appeared in about forty West End productions as well as working in repertory at Birmingham, Nottingham and York. When, in December 1945, the Rank Organisation set up the famous 'charm school' in London, Molly Terraine left Worthing to take charge. Verney was appointed artistic director of the Overture Players, a post he held with great distinction for five years.

Earlier, to celebrate their first anniversary at the Connaught, Verney had directed Ibsen's *Hedda Gabler*, also playing the role of Eilert Loevborg. The title role was not played by a 'guest star' but by Margaret Diamond, the company's leading lady. Margaret Diamond was probably the epitome of weekly repertory actresses of the time. Twenty-nine years old, she was strikingly good-looking, and happier in dramatic rather than comedy roles; she frequently gave outstanding performances and during a long career appeared with every leading repertory company in the country. Her forays into the West End invariably attracted good notices but she had the unhappy knack of being cast in plays that flopped. Like many other actresses, she had a strong affection for Worthing and made many appearances at the Connaught throughout the next thirty years.

During 1945 a regular first-nighter at the Connaught was an RAF officer stationed at Poling, a small village just outside Arundel. Before the war Melville Gillam, as a young man, had run his own tiny shack of a theatre at Lye, on the outskirts of the Midlands town of Stourbridge. On his arrival in Sussex he made himself known to both the management and the company. When, in August, the director booked to stage *The Wind and the Rain* pulled out at the last moment Gillam, at Verney's suggestion, took a week's leave and stepped into the breach.

Anna Turner, who played a leading role, remembered the production as a near disaster: Gillam had mistaken a gentle comedy for high drama. He had taken the title literally and the action was accompanied by the sounds of a roaring gale and torrential rain. 'He was a very kind man and loved by everyone,' she recalled, 'but the cast realised he knew nothing about directing and so we created our own characters and just followed the moves he gave us.' Nevertheless, it was a significant move for Gillam and for Worthing.

When the war in Europe came to an end a new era seemed to have dawned. There was money to be spent, people wanted entertainment and the Connaught could provide it. At last people could take holidays again,the street lights were back on and that summer the town began a boom period. Young actors were being released from the Forces and one of the first to find his way to Worthing was Robin Bailey. He was not new to the stage, having worked for a couple of the Harry Hanson companies before being called up. So impressive was he in his Connaught debut as the Polish airman in Rattigan's *Flare Path* that when, the following week, he was cast in Priestley's *Dangerous Corner* a theatre-goer stopped him in the street to congratulate him on the speed with which he had perfected his English!

The detestable Mollie Terraine rehearsing two members of the Overture Players in 1945

The Connaught's reputation was spreading amongst London managements once again and when the young Peter Ustinov saw one of the shows he signed up Bailey and some other members of the company for minor roles in a film he was about to make. Although the Overture Players acted as a training ground for Rank's contracted film starlets they were in the minority and the management was quite happy to release the others for film work when it came up so Bailey had five weeks away from Worthing filming *Top Secret.*

Although the intention had been to send 'starlets' to Worthing for experience, the process worked in reverse for one actress. Gwen Clark had been a member of the company for several months when she had a week off to work as an 'extra' in a film. She was spotted by Sydney Box who changed her name to Jane Hylton and made her into a hot property. Her subsequent appearances at the Connaught were as a star guest player.

For the more experienced actors the arrival of a contract 'starlet' for a couple of weeks or so was a considerable disruption. Their knowledge of stagecraft was frequently rudimentary and the idea of projecting across the footlights was alien - they were used to the camera zooming in on their reactions. Most of the older members of the company, however, in true theatrical tradition, passed on their knowledge and advice to the youngsters without rancour, exasperating though it must have been at the time. At his debut, not only did Christopher Lee overact outrageously but he had no idea of how to put on make-up. With the help of one of the old hands he soon learned.

Some of the youngsters were so unhappy when they faced a live audience and realised their inadequacies that they got out of the profession as quickly as they could.

Sometimes tempers were not restrained. During the first night of *Charley's Aunt* the director, Molly Terraine, was so incensed at Pete Murray's performance that she

Willard Stocker's production of The Taming of the Shrew *was designed by Anthony Waller. Standing centre stage is Robin Bailey as Petruchio*

took a lipstick and scrawled across his dressing-room mirror 'Get better soon - and I am not referring to your health.'

Terraine's departure for the 'charm school' was greeted with delight by the Worthing company. She was remembered by all as a vicious dragon who sat through rehearsals wearing a hat decorated with a bunch of cherries; her temper could be judged by the degree to which the cherries were shaking.

When Bailey returned to the Connaught after filming, in the spring of 1946, it was to join a new permanent company which was beginning to take shape: led by Margaret Diamond, it included Gwen Cherrell, Ann Castle, Alan Bridges and Charles Morgan. Morgan's career had begun carrying a spear at the Old Vic but he had graduated to more important roles when he made his first appearance at the Connaught in 1937. Now he had been brought in for five weeks whilst Bailey was away: he stayed eight years.

Many other youngsters coming out of the services joined the company, some for just one show, others for much longer, and together with the 'starlets' they formed a formidable 'roll call'. Playing roles both large and small were such names as June Whitfield, Michael Goodliffe, Guy Rolfe, Anthony Steele, Donald Houston, Michael Bates, Barbara Murray, Diana Dors and Petula Clark. Kenneth Williams played one week with the Overture Players, but the town did not impress him; when invited to return for another role he declined, noting in his diary, 'dreadful place, Worthing'.

Melville Gillam was released from the RAF that winter and became the Connaught's House Manager, starting a connection that was to last twenty-two years.

Another ex-serviceman coming to Worthing on demobilisation from the RAF was Willard Stoker, who proved himself an exceptionally fine director. Although he had begun his career as an actor, he was one of those few who had totally abandoned playing in favour of directing. Slim, almost elfin-like, he possessed a remarkable sense of comic inventiveness which showed through in many of his productions. After a few months at the Connaught he became Director of Productions at Birmingham Repertory Theatre and from 1951 to 1962 he was the director of the Liverpool Playhouse. He and Gillam became good friends and Stoker came back to the Connaught on many future occasions. His most outstanding production in the early days was *The Taming of the Shrew,* in which the 'Sly' scenes were set in the present time whilst the remainder was in the Georgian period.

It could almost be said that the Connaught was the forerunner of the 'directors' theatre', for in all the press advertising, where only guest players were named, the director was given prominence every week. Many of them became influential in the theatre of the fifties and later: as well as Stoker, they included Warren Jenkins, Michael Finlayson and Peter Streuli, who directed many outstanding productions at the Arts Theatre Club.

It was between seasons at the Arts that a favourite from the Bell-Fraser days paid a return visit to Worthing. Dorothy Primrose had received a succession of glowing notices for her performances opposite Alec Clunes, the actor-director of the Arts. She came back to the Connaught in May, 1946, to take the leading role in a revival of *Rebecca* and was impressed by the company, particularly the young actor playing Jack Flavell. She was due to return to the Arts to start rehearsals of a prestigious British Council-backed six-month tour of Europe in a classical repertoire. Knowing that Clunes had not completed casting some of the leading roles she recommended Robin Bailey to him and so another Worthing actor got a notable step up in his career. Clunes was impressed by the standard of the Overture Players and subsequently engaged many of the Worthing actors and directors for productions at the Arts.

Shortly after Stoker departed for Birmingham there was another significant change at the Connaught. Percy Busby, who had been licensee and General Manager of the theatre for four years, resigned suddenly. There was no need to search far for a replacement, for Melville Gillam happily accepted promotion.

If the Connaught was a bit thin on guest players in 1946 the situation was reversed the following year with appearances by some very 'big names' of the time. Jill Balcon - a fine actress, now rather better known as the mother of Daniel Day Lewis - was followed by Gordon Jackson, Andrew Crawford, Jane Barrett and Dermot Walsh.

Walsh was an experienced actor before becoming a contract artiste with the Rank Organisation: 'I had come to films from the stage, having graduated from the Abbey Theatre School in Dublin and completed a three-year engagement at the Dublin Gate Theatre, where I played leading juvenile in a classical repertoire.

'I had spent over a year at the studios acting to the camera and I greatly missed the stage, but Rank had a schedule of film projects in development and would not release me for the several months needed for a tour or a West End production. I had only three or four weeks free between films.

'Margaret Lockwood came up with the solution - Worthing Repertory, where each production was completed in twelve days from first rehearsal to the last night's final curtain.

'In 1947 I had March free. It was arranged by Rank that I should appear at the Connaught playing Yank in *The Hasty Heart*. I was not previously acquainted with the horrors of weekly repertory. In Dublin I was used to each production running for at least three weeks after 72 hours' rehearsal and two dress rehearsals held on the two days prior to the opening night. At the Connaught we had just twelve hours rehearsing and one dress rehearsal on the afternoon of the first performance. The resident company, even with that meagre preparation were able to deliver miracles of near-improvised characterisation and performance. I regarded them with wonder and admiration.'

Walsh stayed on for what turned out to be the highlight of 1947, Michael Finlayson's production of *The Merchant of Venice,* for which there was the usual extra week's rehearsal.

'Repertory Players Excel Themselves,' headlined the *Sussex Daily News*, continuing, 'no play has been better done since they started on their Connaught career over three years ago.' Another Rank star, the Burmese actor Abraham Sofaer, who had just played opposite David Niven in the hugely successful film *Matter of Life and Death,* was Shylock. 'Brilliant acting by Abraham Sofaer raises... the production well above the average for a repertory company. His lead obviously inspires the rest of the cast,' wrote the Worthing Gazette. Walsh played Bassanio and Peggy Thorpe-Bates was Portia. One Shakespeare lover, then aged eighteen, remembered it almost fifty years later as one of the finest productions of the play which he had ever seen.

Despite the 'horror of weekly repertory' Dermot Walsh returned to Worthing for a couple of other productions the following year.

Plays by Bernard Shaw were still popular, *Man and Superman* and a revival of *Arms and the Man* doing excellent business. But although there were still plenty of current West End plays to draw on as the basis of the 1947 programme, Verney took to reviving previous successes and, in addition to *Arms and the Man*, *The Corn is Green, Ten Little Niggers* and *Ten Minute Alibi* were given a second showing. One of several highlights was the first staging at the Connaught since the Bragg-Liddell season in 1932 of a classic comedy, *The School for Scandal.* In the height of summer a fine production of Eugene O'Neill's *Ah! Wilderness* played to unexpectedly good business.

Although television was in its infancy - it had returned in the London area the previous June - 1947 proved a difficult year for many repertories. It had been an exceptionally cold winter: snow fell for weeks, there were fuel and food shortages, the euphoria of the immediate post-war days had worn off and money was no longer plentiful. The costs of running a repertory had risen to well over £750 a week and economies had to be made. Gillam's major saving was replacing the expensive pit orchestra by two pianos to provide the interval music.

The Rank Organisation, however, reaffirmed its belief in using repertory as a training ground by financing Ronald Kerr who took over the New Theatre, Bromley. Seating 902 it was almost exactly the same size as the Connaught.

At Worthing a new pattern was beginning to emerge, possibly unintentionally, but highly suitably for a holiday resort: the 'meatier' plays appeared early and late in the year, leaving light comedies and thrillers to cater for the summer visitors. The earlier months of 1948 saw such plays as *She Stoops to Conquer, An Inspector Calls, Heartbreak House* and *Mary Rose*, and it was decided to celebrate the fourth anniversary of the company's opening in Worthing by performing the year's Shakespeare in June.

After the acclaim for the previous year's *Merchant,* Guy Verney persuaded Patricia Burke to play Rosalind in *As You Like It.* A big star of the musical stage, she had just made a very successful transition to the classics. Her visit to Worthing came a couple of weeks after an outstanding season at the Old Vic, in which her roles had included Katherine in *The Taming of the Shrew* and Doll Common in *The Alchemist*. Celia was played by Carol Marsh, who had just made a name for herself playing opposite Richard Attenborough in the film of *Brighton Rock*. This was a return to Worthing for her as she had first come to the Connaught two years earlier as a contract starlet. Amongst the unknown supporting players were Tony Britton, Paul Eddington and Christopher Lee. 'It was my professional debut,' Britton recalled, 'and although Paul and Chris had done some stage work before, none of us had been to drama school; but the three of us were bursting with enthusiasm. We were all determined to make names for ourselves and luck was on our side for we all did it.'

The autumn saw Bridie's *Storm in a Teacup*, *The Apple Cart, The Linden Tree* and Arthur Miller's *All My Sons* (whose London production had been directed by Warren Jenkins shortly after he left Worthing) as well as lighter fare such as *The Man Who Came to Dinner*.

Christmas shows presented a problem for the Overture Players: an adaptation of *Alicein Wonderland* in 1945 was followed a year later with a home-grown pantomime, *Aladdin,* and then in 1947 the Alec Guinness version of *Great Expectations* was staged. From then on, like Bell and Fraser for a while, outside managements were brought in to put on a pantomime.

In the autumn of 1948 a festival of British repertory was mounted at London's St. James's Theatre. Four provincial companies appeared, each for a fortnight: weekly repertories were excluded on the grounds that their standards were not high enough. From Birmingham, Willard Stoker staged a modern dress version of *The Rivals*. All the major roles were taken by actors who, like Stoker, had graduated to Birmingham from Worthing, including Robin Bailey, Gwen Cherrell, Dorothy Wheatley, Rosamund Burne and Ian McNaughton.

Peter Byrne, Paul Eddington and Kenneth Laird in J.B.Priestley's Dangerous Corner

There had, by this time, been a minor renaissance in British theatre. Among the clutter of bedroom farce, drawing-room comedy, teacup drama and puny whodunnits had come interesting new plays, particularly from America and France. Works by Arthur Miller, Tennessee Williams and Jean-Paul Sartre were making their way to London and, ultimately, to provincial repertory.

Shaw's writing was past its prime; Noel Coward, too, was not to repeat sublime comedies like *Blithe*

Spirit, Hay Fever and *Present Laughter*, but Terence Rattigan had moved on from light-hearted aristocratic pieces to the finely drawn drama of *The Browning Version*. Priestley was still writing outstanding plays. But theatre remained primarily in commercial hands; subsidy via the Arts Council was limited.

The Overture Players, although their programming was predominantly 'safe', were prepared to take risks at times, certainly more frequently than Bell and Fraser had dared. Since theatre-going was still a habit, many seats were booked on a 'permanent' basis, and audiences were prepared to take an occasional chance on something like Sartre's *Crime Passionel.* Had the proportion of daring productions been too high, however, there was the danger that audiences would drift away.

At a dinner given by the Theatre Club, proposing the toast to 'the Connaught Theatre', the Chairman, praising the high standard of the Overture Players, commented 'We arrive Monday after Monday, thinking they cannot possibly keep it up. We go away Monday after Monday finding that they have.'

Undoubtedly Rank's money helped. Rosemary Harris, who had been at the Roof Garden Theatre, the home of weekly rep in Bognor Regis, put in four weeks as an unpaid assistant stage manager at the Connaught before going to drama school. 'I think the standard at Bognor was probably just as good,' she said, 'but it was the Rank name that brought the London agents and managers to see the Worthing shows.'

During 1949 Congreve's *Love for Love* did bring complaints to the local press of immorality and unwholesomeness but *Macbeth*, the Sartre and a Chinese piece, *Lady Precious Stream,* played to capacity houses. There were also one or two new plays though only *Lace on her Petticoat,* by Aimee Stuart, achieved any success outside Worthing - and it was Willard Stoker who directed the

The Playgoers Club annual dinner dance at Warnes Hotel

Melville Gillam with visiting star Dennis Price

production at London's Ambassadors Theatre. Visiting players that year included Sally Ann Howes, Maxwell Reed, Hazel Court and Dennis Price, who told the audience at his first performance, 'Worthing should be very proud of its charming and talented repertory company. It is a privilege to appear in Worthing.

Then, suddenly, in the autumn of 1949, everything was about to change.

The Connaught might be doing well but the Rank Organisation's film empire was in dire trouble, revealing a staggering loss of almost four and a half million pounds, brought about largely by government interference and a pernicious Entertainments Tax which was a far higher imposition on cinema than on stage productions.

Savings had to be made. The Charm School was closed and since the Overture Players' lease on the Connaught would expire the following May it was decided that their headquarters should be transferred to Bromley. Ronald Kerr left the New Theatre and Guy Verney moved to Kent although he still had control of productions at Worthing.

Many men, knowing that in six months' time they could be out of a job, would have started looking for another; but Gillam was determined to take over the theatre himself. When he enquired about a lease he was told that Carl Seebold, who was now well into his seventies, had decided to put the Connaught on the market.

Nothing better could have happened for Worthing or for Gillam.

CHAPTER SIX

Apart from a short lead in the *Worthing Herald* hoping for a continuation of the existing policy, the impending sale of the Connaught caused little concern or speculation among the Worthing public. Repertory was an established and, apparently, profitable business: it was inconceivable that it would not continue.

In fact, several companies were interested in the sale but not all for the continuation of repertory. Twice-nightly variety was still popular and one prospective purchaser had this in mind; others had no interest in keeping the Connaught as a theatre at all.

Gillam was quietly working towards his aim and had made several strides forward. Throughout his time at the Connaught he had been in the foyer to meet the audience on its way in and again after the show, accepting any brickbats as well as taking praise for the shows: from this he had built up a profile of the most prominent of the regular patrons. A generous man by nature, he was always impecunious at this period of his life and could do nothing about buying the Connaught himself - but he knew the people who could.

Among the audience every Saturday night was William Chapple, a London diamond merchant who had a flat in Worthing. A great theatregoer, he listened to Gillam's suggestion that between them they should approach other enthusiasts to form a consortium to buy the freehold and allow the theatre to continue.

Realising that it might take time to bring a group together and organise the necessary finance, Gillam had contacted Seebold's solicitors as early as January 1950, before the sale was advertised. 'In view of the fact that to negotiate a deal of such magnitude may take several months,' he wrote, 'I suggest that a short lease be granted, so obviating the possibility of the theatre closing. This point, I feel, is very important, as once the theatre is closed the valuable goodwill of the audience, which has been built up over the past six years, will be lost. Also there is the question of the Licence of the theatre - I feel that in view of the tightening up of Theatre Regulations which has become evident over the past year the Justices may ask for certain improvements if there is a break in the continuity. These points appear to me to be very important in ensuring that the goodwill and prestige of the theatre remains unimpaired.'

As it happened, with Chapple's enthusiasm and diplomacy, the consortium was soon formed; not all the members were wealthy but all were theatre-lovers; some were prominent local businessmen, some were widows and pensioners, all wanted repertory to continue in Worthing. A new company, Connaught Theatre (Worthing) Ltd., was registered with Chapple chairing a Board of nine. The freehold was purchased for £36,000 and Gillam was appointed General Manager - a title which before long changed to Managing Director and Production Manager.

No theatre could have been in better hands.

Broadly, the policy of the new company was to continue on the same lines as its predecessor and when, on Monday, 29 May 1950, the newly-formed Worthing Theatre Company first appeared, many people may not have realised that any change had taken place: basically the company was unaltered. In the opening

Nita Moyce, John Bentley and Charles Morgan in William Douglas Home's Master of Arts, *the first production by the Worthing Theatre Company on 29th May 1950. The set was by Nevil Dickin*

production, William Douglas Home's *Master of Arts*, more than half the roles were played by ex-members of the now defunct Overture Players.

Some changes were envisaged: it was hoped that the theatre might be able to attract touring companies and ballet on occasions. It was also intended to redecorate and refurbish in due course, and work was to begin at once on replacing the erratic ventilation system. Little time was lost in making the improvements: the air conditioning was completed during the summer, new lighting was installed in October, the repainting done in November and before the pantomime opened the gaudy act-drop curtain had been replaced. All the work - at no small cost - was carried out without any loss of either rehearsals or performances.

The Overture Players gave their last performance on Saturday, 27 May, in Tennessee Williams's *The Glass Menagerie*. In his farewell programme note, Guy Verney recalled some of the 272 productions by the company, many of the prominent guest stars who had appeared but, above all, the new talent that had been fostered which 'earned for Worthing's theatre its national reputation.' He also commented that by studying the audiences during the five years in command he had got to know their tastes in theatre.

By following Verney's lead Gillam was able to turn the theatre's national reputation into international renown.

In fact the Overture Players were resuscitated only three weeks later when a production booked for Brighton's Theatre Royal was cancelled at the very last minute and *The Glass Menagerie* was revived to fill the gap.

Gillam, or 'Gillie' as he was known to everyone in the theatre, was born in Dudley in 1912. Nineteen years later, on his first visit to London he saw Coward's *Cavalcade* at Drury Lane and was immediately 'hooked' on the theatre: from then on it became his life. His rudimentary education was compensated for by an innate, wheedling business acumen. Only his dropped 'h's' and a multitude of

Melville Gillam relaxing with actor Nicholas Stevenson and (right) the Connaught's Manager, Kenneth Ewing

malapropisms gave away his humble background (he was heard to refer to a rising actress as having the 'aurora of a star' and more than once admired the new 'gherkin' being worn by a friend!).

In many ways he was like his contemporary, 'Binkie' Beaumont, the colossus of the West End. Both knew what audiences wanted, and both had the knack of spotting outstanding talent in actors, directors, designers and writers. Everything had to be of the best, both in their private lives and in their theatres. They each insisted on the highest possible standards of presentation and enforced a rigid discipline on their employees. Both were homosexual. Strangely, though Beaumont's H. M. Tennent organisation took up many of Gillie's discoveries, none of the new plays staged at Worthing transferred to the West End under its banner.

Gillie had total control of the Connaught. He selected the plays, often cast them, engaged the directors, designers, technicians and front-of-house staff, dealt with the advertising and controlled the finances. Chapple and the Board were always there, in the background, to offer advice, support and finance when needed. Realising that, though during his years with the Overture Players he had learnt all he needed to know about the business side of running the Connaught, he was not entirely confident on the artistic side, he asked the Board to appoint Willard Stoker as a part-time artistic adviser for the first four months.

The Connaught became Gillie's life: he rarely took holidays and he soon developed a set routine. His main home was an elegant regency flat in Ambrose Place, yards away from the theatre, and he had a small place in London. Although he gave all the directors a free hand, he would watch the two final rehearsals and the opening performance which would be followed an 'inquest' on the production with everybody involved. Although Gillie's comments were always shrewd and concise, those meetings would often last into the early hours.

The next morning he was on an early train to London to spend Tuesday and Wednesday auditioning, meeting agents, directors, managements and seeing shows.

Jessie Matthews and Charles Morgan in Larger than Life *(1951)*

On Thursday he would arrive at Brighton in time for the matinee at the Theatre Royal, then it was back to Worthing to catch up on what had happened during his absence. The remainder of the week was spent immersed in Connaught affairs and, although he tried to take Sundays off, the evening was usually passed dining with the Chapples, frequently being joined by senior members of the company.

Short, dapper and always immaculately dressed, he was very shy and, to those outside the theatrical fraternity, appeared a very private person. To his friends he had a great sense of fun and was always ready for a celebration, especially if it involved the company in some way. He was generous, a great entertainer and was always loyal to anyone who had helped him but he could be viperish.

His devotion to the Connaught was admired by everyone, even if some of the circle could not like him. Many young actresses coming into the company found him difficult. Pauline Yates, in her second job, felt he was a martinet who thought he was God. On the other hand, Charles Morgan, who had known him since his arrival at the Connaught, and Hazel Bainbridge, an older actress, both got on well with him.

Elizabeth Spriggs had the greatest respect for him. 'It was', she said, 'his insistence on the very highest of standards at all times which made the Connaught so successful.' Josephine Tewson recalled that wherever she went in repertory things were wrong - names were misspelt in the programme, clothes not quite in period, but never at Worthing: 'Gillie was a stickler for getting every detail just right.' If he found something he did not approve of, out would come one of his most frequently used expression, 'We're too close to London, ducky, to get away with that.' (The other was the instruction he gave to everyone who joined the company - 'Keep it West End, keep it West End.')

He demanded that on or off stage his company must be immaculate at all times. Unless the part called for it, he would not allow his actresses to wear chain-store frocks on stage - they had to 'dress above' the ladies in the audience. Although the girls were allowed to wear slacks at rehearsals, if they left the theatre, even to pop across the road to post a letter, they had to change into a skirt. For a costume play the clothes would be the best that could be hired. If, at dress rehearsal, he spotted a loose hem he would be up on stage with a needle, repairing the damage himself, a habit which did not endear him to everyone.

'He was a fusspot but devoted to theatre,' commented Warren Mitchell.

He was just as strict with the male members of the company - Michael Bryant was sacked for fraternising with one of the young chorus girls in pantomime, although re-engaged a couple of years later. But this discipline engendered a sense of respect for each other amongst the company: at rehearsal or in performance everybody would help each other to give of their best and worked as a team. 'It was a civilised and, yes, "cultured" company,' said Hazel Bainbridge, while Willard Stoker kept on being drawn back purely because of 'everybody's enthusiasm'.

Alfred Burke recalled Gillie's ability to make the company feel that they were wanted and valued and liked. 'I was charmed by this man who made me feel that I was a member of an exclusive club and that I would always be welcome. He could, of course, show a little steel when it became appropriate but it always ended amicably. Gillie was good.'

The first resident director of productions was Jordan Lawrence, an experienced man of the theatre, both as a director and a writer, who got the new company off to a flying start. On his departure in the autumn, Michael Finlayson returned for a while.

Gillie knew the attraction to audiences of bringing in guest stars and for the third production he persuaded local resident and still glamourous musical comedy star of the twenties and thirties, Elsie Randolph, to come out of retirement to take the lead in *Two Dozen Red Roses,* a lightweight piece which demanded (and got) a dynamic performance in the leading role.

The following week, with a revival of *Romeo and Juliet*, Carol Marsh, the impressive Celia of two years earlier, returned to play Juliet. The Romeo was a regular and popular member of the company, Ronald Lewis, who, very shortly after, went on to play leads with the Old Vic company. In supporting roles in the production were Alec McCowen and a young actor called Warren Missell - it was during his stay in Worthing that he became Warren Mitchell. In August, Lupino Lane appeared in one of his great successes, *Twenty to One,* a production which brought to the Connaught Disley Jones who was to become one of its most distinguished designers.

As had become usual, light-hearted fare was provided during the height of the summer but that autumn, apart from a revival of Shaw's *Mrs. Warren's Profession,* there was little 'meat' in the diet.

At Christmas Gillam continued to 'bring in' pantomime but he changed managements, insisting that the cast should include at least one well-known name. Alan Crooks put on *Mother Goose* in which he cast a top variety and cabaret artiste, Phyllis Robins, as principal boy. The title role was taken by one of the new wave of up and coming comedians, Arthur Haynes, playing his first 'dame'. Several members of the rep were in supporting roles. But it was a rather typical provincial pantomime, a hastily put on bit of tat.

The following February the new management fulfilled one promise by booking the Ballet Rambert for a week, which at that time, toured with a full orchestra and corps-de-ballet. The response was incredible: every performance was sold out and each day about 500 people were turned away. It was hardly surprising that the company was booked for a return visit later the same year. Another successful innovation was to vary the programme with a week or two of the popular seaside summer show, *The Fol-de-Rols.* On the first visit they played to packed houses for a week in June, even though the town's resident summer attraction had already opened at the pier with Bill Fraser leading the company.

The first year of the new company had proved very successful in every direction. It was a time when some particularly notable plays were being staged in London and Worthing's productions of *Home at Seven*, *The Heiress, Harvey* and *Streetcar Named Desire* played to capacity audiences. With production costs rising, Gillam knew that it was time for Worthing to try out some new plays. One benefit was that the top London managements sent representatives to see provincial 'try outs', which, in turn, was an incentive for more experienced actors to work outside the West End. The main benefit, however, was that if a play made a successful transfer to Shaftesbury Avenue, the royalties for the rep could be a very valuable source of additional income.

Worthing audiences viewed the move with suspicion. After a dramatic decline in attendance for the first premiere he staged, Gillam decided that the big names would have to be employed if he wanted good houses for future new productions.

For his second attempt he found a play by an established author, Guy Bolton, and called in a strong cast headed by Robert Beatty, Dinah Sheridan and Alan MacNaughton while Willard Stoker came back to direct. *The Long Arm* was a light piece of entertainment and if it went no further, it kept Worthing audiences happy and the stars filled the theatre.

A few years earlier one of the first post-war film successes had been *The Blue Lamp.* Its author, Ted Willis, decided to adapt the story for the stage. Gillam felt that the well-known name of *The Blue Lamp* was not a sufficiently fool-proof

Margaret Tyzack making her debut appearance with the Worthing Theatre Company in 1954. Alongside her in The Orchard Walls *are Charles Morgan, Anne Bishop and Hazel Bainbridge*

attraction for the Connaught and so for the role of the police sergeant (forerunner of *Dixon of Dock Green)* George Curzon came to Worthing and Patrick Doonan played the young criminal, the part that, on screen, had made a star of Dirk Bogarde. Sergeant Dixon's young side-kick, Andy Crawford, was played by a member of the resident company, Peter Byrne, a role he repeated on television for many years. After its try-out at Worthing, the Jack Hylton management staged the play, taking it on tour for four weeks before a seventeen-week summer season at Blackpool. It then transferred to the London Hippodrome and although the London run survived only 32 performances, overall it made a tidy sum for the Connaught.

Nancy Price as Nurse Cavell with Hazel Bainbridge and John Dearth. The production was designed by Disley Jones

One of Gillam's greatest flairs and certainly one of the greatest assets for the Connaught was his ability to see in a young actor that spark which takes him to the top of his profession. Michael Bryant, Margaret Tyzack, Ian Holm, Elizabeth Spriggs, Susannah York, Sarah Miles, Daniel Massey, John Standing, John le Mesurier, Patricia Routledge, Gerald Flood, Vivienne Merchant, Terence Alexander, Anthony Bate, Caroline Blakiston, Dinsdale Lansden, Andrew Sachs, Clive Francis and Nigel Hawthorne are just a few examples of the quality of actor that Gillam had as resident members of his company. Not that he was always right: when one young hopeful approached him for a job he refused even to audition her on the grounds that 'no one could expect to be taken seriously as an actress with the name "Maggie Smith".'

Sonia Dresdel starred in the 1953 premiere of Piccolo *with Charles Morgan and John le Mesurier*

Another gift he had was to give the Worthing public what it wanted for so long. A pleasant theatre, a sound play, first class sets, a good bar for the interval and polished performances made for an ideal evening out - which is what the Connaught provided week in and week out. West End successes, the daring risk of a new play now and then, the spice of an occasional 'name' and the now regular visits of the Ballet Rambert and *The Fol-de-Rols* kept audiences happy and the box office busy.

The Theatregoers' Club was very important to Gillam, and many well-known personalities in the theatre world accepted his invitation to talk to the Sunday meetings. During 1951 the young author of a new book came to address the Club. As soon as the two met they were attracted to each other. As well as being a writer, Gillam's new friend was assistant to Harold Fielding. Fielding had given up playing the violin for a living and was now an agent as well as a leading promoter of concerts and light entertainment. There began a business relationship between the Fielding organisation and the Connaught which was to be mutually beneficial for the next fifteen years.

In 1952 the idea of having a touring production in for a week was tried but, unfortunately, despite an excellent cast which included Irene Browne, Adrienne Allen, Irene Handl and Peter Cushing - paying his first visit to Worthing since making a name for himself - the play was poor and audiences, although good, felt they were happier with plays and actors they were used to. There was some outstanding work by the local company that year with such diverse productions as *Ring Round the Moon, The Lady's Not for Burning* with Jean Kent, Cocteau's *The Eagle Has Two Heads* and Pinero's classic *The Second Mrs. Tanqueray.*

Undoubtedly the crowning glory of the year was to get Donald Wolfit to join the company in *Othello*. Wolfit had played the role on ninety-two occasions with his own, now disbanded, company. When Gillam heard that Wolfit's ambition was to turn that ninety-two into a century he suggested it could be done with a week at Worthing. Two favourites of the company at that time, John Dearth and Ann Castle, played Iago and Desdemona, with another guest, Sheila Burrell, as Emilia. Two weeks of rehearsal under the direction of Jack Williams - who had become resident director - and costumes hired from Stratford-upon-Avon. The week was a resounding success but it was the last time that Shakespeare was played at the Connaught for nine years.

Gillam had been less fortunate in trying to get another 'heavyweight' to Worthing, the fine Czech actor, Frederick Valk. A date was agreed for him to appear in Eugene O'Neill's *Anna Christie* but a month before rehearsals were due to begin Valk was offered a West End role and asked to be released from the Worthing contract.

Seebold had died in November 1951, and early in the following year his executors asked Gillam if the Connaught would be interested in buying the old Connaught Hall. Apart from a few amateur shows, it had been largely unused since the Home Guard's productions until November 1945, when a new company transformed it into the Ritz Ballroom. This flourished for a year or two but by the autumn of 1950 it had failed.

The Board agreed that the space could be an asset to the Connaught as a design studio or rehearsal space, for storage or even for letting.

Pantomime worried Gillam. Alan Crooks had put in a couple but they were not of a very high standard, nor had the scripts been very good. Gillam knew how to put on a play in a week but pantomime was more complicated and needed longer preparation: yet Crooks, like many other provincial pantomime managements, frequently had no more than four days of rehearsals. The Connaught's shallow stage also made it difficult to accommodate sets that had been hired in from much larger theatres. Now that the old hall was available to build sets and make dozens of costumes Gillam wanted the theatre to produce its own Christmas shows. When

Terence Rattigan's The Deep Blue Sea *was one of many Connaught productions in which Ann Castle took the leading female role in 1953. She is seen here with Norman Scace and Richard Coleman*

Chapple and he discussed the idea, Gillam put forward the one major doubt in his mind: ever since it was invented pantomime has been a big money-maker for theatres, but it requires a huge investment and occasionally, perhaps through bad weather, a truly lousy show or an epidemic - only two Christmases earlier Brighton had been in the grip of a smallpox outbreak - instead of a large profit there is an enormous loss. If this happened at Worthing the repertory could be put at risk. Chapple solved the problem by setting up a separate company, C. T. (Productions) Ltd., which he financed himself, to float the Christmas show.

The first 'home-grown' pantomime was *Cinderella*, staged at Christmas 1952. Gillam had formed a strong relationship with both the *Fol-de-Rols* management and the Ballet Rambert who both gave invaluable help. The musical director, Harry Tait, and the choreographer, Thurza Rogers, came from the *Fol-de-Rols* and making her stage debut in the chorus was Doreen Wells, later to become prima ballerina of the Royal Ballet. The bulk of the cast consisted of the rep company, but artistes from the world of variety and concert party came in as principals - at this early stage they were of the second rank but later it would be big names who spent Christmas in Worthing. The production was in the hands of the resident director, Jack Williams, and all the twelve sets and the dozens of costumes were made by the Connaught staff.

After the pantomime Gillam took advantage of having Harry Tait and Thurza Rogers around to stage the theatre's first musical. *The Two Bouquets* provided a good opening for what turned out to be a very good year indeed. Following its success in Worthing, a few months later *The Two Bouquets* was revived at the St Martin's Theatre in a production directed by Willard Stoker.

It was Coronation year and Gillam gave the town one or two things out of the ordinary. The Clifford Odets drama, *Winter Journey*, Fry's *A Phoenix too Frequent* and Nancy Price in a revival of *Nurse Cavell.* In March Fay Compton appeared as a guest in a play with a religious theme, *Family Tree,* prompting *The Stage* newspaper to write in a leader:

PRESTIGE

'The growing practice of actors accepting the invitation of repertory theatres to play as guest artistes is to be commended and it is hoped that more and more artistes will accept such engagements in the future. Now that players of the calibre of Fay Compton and Donald Wolfit have repeated some of their most distinguished performances as repertory guests... at Worthing... others may follow suit without losing prestige. Miss Compton and Mr. Wolfit are still at the peak of their careers....

'Only good should come out of this guest star system. It is good for the artistes themselves to be working and it is good for the company to have a new colleague in their midst. And the public benefit, too, as even the most loyal weekly repertory supporters will enjoy seeing a great theatrical name shed lustre on the cast of familiar players.'

That autumn three regular members of the company, Ann Castle, Charles Morgan and Richard Coleman, gave outstanding performances in both *The Deep Blue Sea* and James Bridie's *Daphne Laureola.* In fact, in less than four months Ann Castle recreated in Worthing roles that had just been played by Sybil Thorndike, Edith Evans, Peggy Ashcroft, Lynn Fontanne and Edwige Feuillère (in the famous tear-jerker, *The Lady of the Camellias* which Castle made genuinely moving) she did not attempt to copy or impersonate these famous actresses but she bore comparison with all of them.

Television was still in its infancy and many homes did not possess a set. Gillam arranged with a local firm, Bowers and Wilkins, for a screen four feet by three feet to be installed and for 6/6d (32p) - including morning coffee and a buffet lunch - the bar was packed to see the relay of the Coronation procession and service.

The following year, 1954, the Connaught really won the respect of London managements for its discovery of new plays. In May Raymond Francis returned to Worthing to play the lead in a new comedy with the unpromising title of *Humpy.* Henry Sherek saw it, re-named it *All for Mary* and took it to the Duke of York's Theatre where it ran for 313 performances.

Almost three months later, on a hot July evening, the curtain rose on yet another first performance and by this time Gillam was beginning to risk opening new plays without star names. On this occasion the lead was being taken by an actress never before seen in Worthing. By the final curtain the audience knew that the Connaught had found another winner, not only in the play but in the actress, too. They were right - the play was *Sailor Beware* and the actress Peggy Mount.

Next morning word spread round the town that there was a very good laugh at the Connaught this week. The box office was besieged and at once Gillam postponed the next production (for which rehearsals were about to begin) and *Sailor Beware* ran for a fortnight.

Sailor Beware became one of the biggest hits of the 1950s, playing over 1,200 performances in London before touring throughout the country and Australia; yet at the beginning it seemed destined to fall by the wayside.

The problems began as soon as Gillam had scheduled it into the Connaught's programme. First Olive Milbourne, a long-standing member of the company who was to play the leading role of Emma Hornett, asked to be released in order to take a small film part. Gillam chased around agents to find a replacement and luckily Peggy Mount, who had been playing a season at Windsor, was available. With Jack Williams on holiday, Andre Van Gyseghem, until recently artistic director of the Nottingham Playhouse, was in charge of the production, and at the first rehearsal declared himself unhappy with some of the casting. Alfred Burke, who had been brought in to play the clergyman who appears only in the last act, suddenly found himself in the major role of Emma Hornett's hen-pecked husband.

Representatives of several London managements were in the first night audience, but it was an independent impresario, Jack Waller, there in person, who struck a deal with the authors, Philip King and Falkland Cary, to buy the rights.

The major problem that Waller faced was persuading a London theatre to bring in a show without any well-known names. He was determined that only Peggy Mount should play the lead but theatre-owner after theatre-owner turned him down, sure that without a 'name' the audience would stay away. Eventually, six months later, the Strand Theatre agreed to Waller staging it there.

Ideally he would have liked to have taken the Worthing production to London unchanged, but Michael Craig, who had originally played Carnoustie Bligh, was filming and Gillam refused to allow both Richard Coleman and Hazel Bainbridge, leading members of the Worthing company, to go to the West End. Waller chose Coleman, who recreated his role of the sailor, Albert. Peggy Mount was very annoyed that Hazel Bainbridge was not to repeat her role of the scatterbrained sister-in-law since they had played off each other so well, but she was in no position to lay down any laws at that stage of her career.

Another problem was that Andre Van Gyseghem was not available to direct. Gillam put himself forward, despite having directed nothing since the disastrous *Wind and the Rain* nine years earlier and there is no doubt that, successful though it was, the production of *Sailor Beware* at the Strand Theatre was nowhere near as strong or as well acted as at the Connaught; but who could have refused a fee of £100 for a two week rehearsal period plus 1½% of the gross takings of a show that ran for three years?

Two more premieres were staged in 1954, one never to be heard of again and the other a dramatic play by the part-author of *Sailor Beware*, Philip King. *Serious Charge* had, in fact, been seen once before, at a Sunday evening performance by the Repertory Players, a London club theatre, the previous year; but this was its first commercial appearance. Although by today's standards its handling of the plight of a country vicar accused of interfering with a young boy would almost certainly be considered trivial, if not trite, it was then daring and delicately handled. A London transfer was inevitable and, by coincidence, it opened at the Garrick Theatre the night after *Sailor Beware* premiered at the Strand Theatre - so three Connaught productions were then running in the West End.

The success of these plays had an immediate effect on the Connaught. Managements crowded to Worthing's first nights to be sure of being able to bid quickly for any future likely hits. Newspaper critics, too, were quick to come from London to review productions. Now even the most established of authors were eager for Worthing to try out their latest efforts, and actors who might have been tempted to stay in London in the hope of getting a television part were anxious to

Jean Kent and Mercy Haystead in She Smiled at Me, *a musical which went straight from the Connaught to the West End where it lasted four performances! The designer was Robert Weaver*

be seen in a new Connaught play. Local audiences began to feel a glow of pride at having been in at the birth of a hit: stars were no longer necessary to ensure an audience for a premiere.

The result was a foregone conclusion: in the following year, 1955, sixteen premieres were staged, sometimes two in succession. Not all of these were totally new plays; by now news of the care with which Worthing staged plays had reached Broadway. Sigmund Miller, whose *One Bright Day* had enjoyed a successful run in New York, insisted that the British premiere should be at the Connaught. Nancy Mitford's adaptation of Anna Bonacci's French success, *The Dazzling Hour*, was a joint production with one of America's top impresarios, Gilbert Miller.

New plays by leading writers Michael Clayton Hutton, Robin Maugham and Keiran Tunney were amongst those staged but it was not a good year for transfers, only three of the sixteen making the trip to London, two of which were total failures.

One of these was the musical version of Tom Robertson's famous Victorian comedy, *Caste*. Scored for a keyboard, it provided a pleasantly light evening and it enjoyed a successful week in October. By coincidence another musical version of the play was being tried out at Windsor the same week. Gillam and C. T. (Productions) Ltd. decided that rather than waste time and let an outside management get their hands on it, they would take their version of it into the West End themselves. The music was re-worked for a full orchestra, Jean Kent was cast in the leading role, there was new choreography and with a new title, *She Smiled at Me*, the revised show opened the 1956 season on 16 January.

The new production was due to move into the St Martin's Theatre at the beginning of the following month, but it was obvious that despite the presence of Jean Kent the new cast needed strengthening. Eight of the twelve roles were recast and after a week's rehearsal *She Smiled at Me* moved into the West End on Thursday, 2 February. It moved out again, after four performances, that Saturday night!

As Ken Turner, then assistant scenic artist, recalled, the Connaught management had not realised the extent to which a West End impresario would have invested in the show. Robert Weaver's designs were excellent but the sets themselves, built in the Connaught studios, were okay for weekly rep but not substantial enough for a London audience - whenever other Connaught productions had been to London the sets had been rebuilt by one of the major theatrical construction companies. The costumes, too, all hired from M. Berman Ltd., one of the top costumiers, were fine for the supporting players but the principals' clothes should have been individually designed and tailored.

As it happened, the most exciting premiere the Connaught staged in 1955 played to very small audiences; but those who did venture to it were rewarded by an unforgettable evening of theatre. Unfortunately, many of the Connaught regulars felt that to spend an evening with one actor standing alone on stage, reciting the words of a rather obscure Welsh poet, would not entertain them. And so Worthing, the envy of so many other theatres, failed to respond to Emlyn Williams as Dylan Thomas.

The policy of new plays continued, however, and in the ten years from 1956 over sixty more were seen, some of which went further, many of which didn't. That May *The Times* revealed that four productions heading for the West End had begun life at the Connaught Theatre, 'which in the last few years has come to be a familiar name with those who take an interest in theatrical signs and portents.'

The delay in transferring a play from a repertory theatre to its London home sometimes had unexpected benefits for the local audience. A few weeks after her success in *Sailor Beware,* Peggy Mount played the autocratic Queen Mother in

The 1954 production of Rattigan's The Sleeping Prince *with Lawrence Davidson, Ann Bishop, Valerie Miller, John Merivale and Peggy Mount. The set was by Rita Taylor*

Despite its shallow stage the Connaught staged spectacular pantomimes with star names at Christmas. Robinson Crusoe *in 1955 featured Lupino Lane, then one of the country's leading 'dames', Shirley Eaton, Lucille Graham and a rising young comedian, Norman Vaughan. All the sets and most of the costumes were made in the theatre. In addition to a cast of twelve principals plus fourteen professional singers and dancers there was a 12 piece band in the orchestra pit*

Rattigan's slight piece, *The Sleeping Prince* - she electrified the play and the audience. In two roles she had convinced Worthing that here was an actress with a much wider range than London was able to appreciate until several years later when she started to appear with the Old Vic and Royal Shakespeare Companies.

Worthing was always pleased to see one of its protégés move on to better things, but their last week at the Connaught was tinged with a touch of sadness; it was like saying 'goodbye' to an old friend and those farewells were invariably accompanied by loads of gifts.

If the Connaught was finding plays and actors, at Christmas it proved it could find comedians as well.

It soon became obvious that despite the shallow stage, the Connaught could put on a spectacular pantomime, complete with the traditional transformation scene.

Local girl and big, big star Alma Cogan returned to Worthing for the 1959 Christmas pantomime, Goldilocks and the Three Bears. *She is seen with David Henderson Tate*

Singers, dancers and comedians, like the orchestra, were imported but the rep players were often given leading roles too. In *Jack and the Beanstalk* props doubled the height of six-feet tall leading actor, Richard Coleman, to make a most imposing giant, but the star of that production was a young comedian who was beginning to be heard on the radio, Terry Scott. A year later Norman Vaughan was the lead comedian while, in 1956, a completely unknown name, Ted Rogers, made a first class Buttons in *Cinderella* - four years later he played the role at London's Adelphi Theatre. In that Worthing production of *Cinderella* a poodle was played by Ian Holm, the orchestra was conducted by Ron Grainer and the director was David Croft - the man behind TV's *Dad's Army* and *Are You Being Served?*

The relationship between Gillam and the Harold Fielding organisation was growing closer and they were giving a great deal of help in casting the Christmas productions. Largely through them many big names of variety, radio and, later, television came to the Connaught for the pantomime season.

Stars like Elsie and Doris Waters, Lupino Lane, Douglas Byng, Shirley Eaton, Alma Cogan, the Beverley Sisters, Anne Shelton, Mark Wynter and Donald Peers all appeared in the Christmas shows. For many years the pantomimes made substantial profits which were ploughed back into the weekly repertory productions.

By 1955 Gillam had taken the Connaught to the highest peaks of provincial weekly repertory and had proved, moreover, that, although hard work, it did not have to be synonymous with the second rate. The productions were polished, immaculately staged and, if the cast had to resort to tricks of technique, these were not obvious to the audience nor was the voice of the assistant stage manager's prompt heard.

CHAPTER SEVEN

Life in weekly repertory was hard and the hours were long.

The linchpin and possibly hardest worker was not Gillam but the director. Guy Vaesen had that role at the Connaught for six years.

'One of my lucky streaks has been that I've always been a light sleeper, usually awake and reading soon after 5.00 am. so there was no problem about reading a play a day. Casting them was fairly simple, as we had a reasonably large permanent company and one did one's best to interleave large parts with minor ones. I was extremely lucky with most of my designers and we had frequent chats together before he got down to the business of offering a design. As for rehearsals, I was usually rid of my correspondence well before starting time at 10.00 am. Working with a resident company I frequently conducted my moves with a wave of an arm or a beckoning of a suggestion to sit and so on. I tried to be thorough in editing and cutting before rehearsals began.' (Derek Fowlds called him a martinet. 'Of course I was. How else get on a play in a week that had any semblance of originality?')

The cast assembled on Tuesday morning to read through the following week's play; they would then see a ground plan of the settings. After lunch the director would give the cast their moves and they would break between 5.00 and 5.30 to grab a quick meal before the evening performance. Most plays at that time were written in three acts, act one was rehearsed on Wednesday morning, finishing in good time for the afternoon matinee which began at 2.30. Thursday morning was devoted to rehearsing act two which was followed by a dash to the noticeboard where the cast list for the following week's production would have gone up. Thursday afternoon was free for the cast to concentrate on learning their lines. On Friday morning the third act was rehearsed and after lunch the whole play was run through. On Saturday morning there was an uninterrupted, final run-through in front of Gillam when everyone had to be word perfect. Sunday was a day of rest, though before Monday afternoon clothes had to be chosen, cleaned and ironed and study of the lines for the following week had to begin. For the ladies Monday morning was spent at a local hairdressing salon where, generously, the proprietor provided them with a light lunch. The sole dress rehearsal began at 2.30 on Monday afternoon and the curtain was up on the first performance five hours later.

The normal rehearsal schedule could be thrown into confusion when the current production was a new play. Re-writes were commonplace and new lines had to be learnt and moves redesigned in breaks between rehearsals for the next production - changes to the script of *Humpy* were made after each of the eight performances!

Until 1948 there was no agreed contract for members of a repertory company. Some managers, like Bell and Fraser, had been generous with payment, others had not. All worked on the basis that there was no payment for rehearsals, no paid holidays, no sick pay and all clothes, other than period costumes, had to be provided by the players at their own expense. Now, however, there was a standard contract which provided a minimum wage for actors of £4.10.0d a week for eight performances. No actor receiving less than £6 a week had to provide more than two

Two 'typical' Connaught sets built and painted within a week: Michael Eve's design for Cecil Madden's Loophole *(1957), with Elizabeth Spriggs, Kenneth Laird and John Merivale, and below:* Subway in the Sky, *designed by Robert Weaver with (seated) Gerald Flood and Patricia Routledge*

'ordinary walking suits' and one evening suit, while an actress on less than £8 had to provide only two day dresses and one evening gown. Above these rates all reasonable modern clothes had to be provided. No member of the Connaught company was on the Equity minimum - most were on much more. This agreement made no mention of technical staff nor the young assistant stage managers who could also be called on to play small parts when necessary.

Meanwhile the backroom boys had been working on the sets - on the rare occasions when there was only one, it seemed almost like a holiday! Apart from reading the plays and designing them, the scenic artist, with the help of one assistant and two carpenters, had to build and paint the scenery. This consisted of a series of heavy wooden frames with canvas stretched across them. Eighteen feet high, they could be anything from one to six feet wide. These were loaded onto a frame which occupied the whole of the back wall of the stage. Painting could not be done whilst a show was on and so the designer and his assistant could only work during the day or late at night. It was also down to the designer, in conjunction with the stage manager, to select and organise all the furnishings, carpets, curtains and props that the production needed, to be begged, borrowed or hired from local suppliers. If it was a period play the designer had to find time to go to a London costumier to select costumes for the cast.

For them the real work began when the curtain fell on Saturday night's show. The current sets and furnishings had to be dismantled and moved out of the theatre and the following week's brought in and assembled. In an article in *Sightline*, the Journal of Theatre Technology and Design, Disley Jones recalled his weekends at the Connaught: 'From 10.30 on Saturday night until 7.30 on Monday evening you just worked on and on. When we could find them, there were Purple Hearts. If we couldn't get those we resorted to Benzedrine inhalers. At four in the morning we would retire to the Green Room and make lemon tea and well away on a high we would carry on painting until breakfast time when an incredulous stage staff would come in to find we had worked non-stop through the night. Our sophisticated drug taking was a close secret.'

On Monday morning the technical details of lighting and sound effects were prepared for the afternoon rehearsal. Yet the first performance at Worthing was very often more polished than the final performance of some fortnightly reps.

How was it done? Nobody would dream of putting up with those conditions today, yet everybody who went through the treadmill of weekly repertory at Worthing has fond recollections as well as dread moments.

Rehearsing a previously produced play was comparatively easy, the published acting editions having been based on the original prompt script. This would include descriptions of the characters, the moves used in the original production as well as photographs and ground plans of the sets, furniture and property lists and a lighting plot.

A new play would depend very much on the director: the good ones could get to the heart of it at once and know, almost instinctively, how it should be played and which were the crucial lines. Being rehearsed by a guest director could be difficult: he would not realise how various members of the company worked. Hazel Bainbridge, for example, was an actress who always held something back for the actual performance and so there were sometimes difficulties in rehearsal.

Inevitably accidents and illness occurred but even though there were no understudies, not one performance was cancelled. If there was time, Gillam would ring round agents and actors he knew to find out if there was anyone available who had played the part before.

Eileen O'Connor and Michael Bryant as mother and son in Ring for Catty, *July 1956*

When this failed it was a question of sending the assistant stage manager, or anybody not playing that week, on to the stage with the 'book' to read the part.

The Connaught's two bar ladies, Hilda Myers and Nancy Ayling, take time off for a drink with Sarah Churchill

On one occasion, Michael Bryant, who had just left the company to start rehearsals for *The Iceman Cometh* at the Arts Theatre, popped in for the first night of a new play only to be collared by Gillam and handed the script. Ten minutes later he was on stage while the leading man was enduring a severe bilious attack. Richard Coleman, who had bought a house in Worthing, was commuting to the Strand Theatre for his part in *Sailor Beware* while his wife, Peggy Sinclair, had retired from the stage to bring up a family. One Wednesday morning the assistant stage manager knocked at the door and handed her the script of Coward's *Private Lives*. The actress playing Amanda had been taken ill, Peggy must take over the role that afternoon. She did, and the experience brought her back to the stage full time.

If the cast worked hard, so did the management. Gillam and his House Manager did all the publicity, arranging the advertising, printing and distribution of posters and programmes. They issued the contracts, dealt with all the correspondence, had tickets printed, ordered the bar and ice cream stocks and did a hundred and one other jobs with the assistance of one part-time secretary.

Although, naturally, actors, designers and directors moved on, other members of the staff, backstage and front of house, remained for years. They, too, worked exceptionally hard. Barbara Howlett, who came to the box office in 1948, ran the operation with just two part-timers and she herself doubled as the management's secretary.

The usherettes, most of whom had arrived in the 1940s, all found themselves making costumes for the pantomimes. The two bar staff not only did the six evenings but morning coffee every day and matinee teas twice a week (they also ran a sweet shop just round the corner from the Connaught). The smartly dressed commissionaire who summoned taxis at the end of the evening performance spent his days in overalls doing general maintenance work.

It was hard work and it was team work. But the continual graft took its toll: at some stage most of the company, like the designers, had to resort to amphetamines to keep going.

Not that everything went smoothly on stage; there were many mishaps but the company used their experience and ingenuity to hide them from the audience.

On one occasion the veteran actor A. E. Mathews was guesting in *The Chiltern Hundreds,* a role he had played around 2,000 times. Suddenly in a scene with Charles Morgan as the butler, Mathews, then 82 years old, lost the thread. 'Damn it,

Lawrence Davidson, Elizabeth Spriggs and Patricia Routledge in A Man About the House. *The 1957 production was designed by Eoin Sprot*

Charles,' he said in full voice, 'I can't recall what I should be saying.' Morgan, remaining in character, gave him the line and there was not even a titter from the audience.

Sarah Miles and Hazel Bainbridge were on stage for the opening scene of one play and as the curtain went up there was silence: this was unknown at the Connaught - there was always a round of applause for the set - but tonight, nothing. When they looked out front they saw that the safety curtain was still in place.

Warren Mitchell, playing Friar Lawrence in *Romeo and Juliet*, had been given some good advice by Reginald Long, one of the older members of the company. Something will always go wrong in Shakespeare, he was told, so learn a speech from any of the plays, it doesn't matter which so long as its not one of the well-known bits. Advice which Mitchell put to good use that week when in full flow he looked into the wings and saw that Carol Marsh as Juliet was having a problem with

Big 'names' made frequent appearances at the Connaught. Always popular whenever they appeared were Sonnie Hale and Elsie Randolph - seen here with Elizabeth Spriggs, Amanda Walker and Daniel Massey in A Nest of Robins, *designed by Robert Weaver*

a costume change. He covered her delayed entrance and said later he doubted whether anyone in the audience realised that in the middle of *Romeo and Juliet* they had listened to a chunk from *Richard II!*

At another performance Mitchell put the rest of the cast on the spot. One thing that brought about Gillam's wrath was to 'corpse' on stage, that is laugh at something that has gone wrong. As Friar Lawrence, Mitchell, over the supposed corpse of Juliet, had the lines 'Dry up your tears, and stick your rosemary/ On this fair corse, and, as the custom is/ In all her best array bear her to church.' Unfortunately he came to a complete halt after 'stick your rosemary' and all he could see were heaving stomachs and tightening facial muscles - in those few words Juliet became a very merry corpse!

Roland Curram remarked that it was the discipline that Gillam instilled in the company that made them all pull together when anything went amiss. 'It might,' he said, 'be your fault next time, so don't give anybody the excuse for not covering for you when it is.' But nobody could help the young Sarah Miles when she made an entry not realising her evening gown had become entangled and she was displaying her left breast!

Not that everybody liked each other: for almost two years Charles Morgan and Ann Castle led the company and on-stage they seemed to be the ideal partnership. Nobody realised they were rarely in harmony, they were just too professional to let it show.

The resident company usually numbered ten but would be reinforced when the play demanded a larger cast: fourteen or sixteen players, sometimes even more, were often needed. In those days the last train back to London left after the curtain came down and actors were happy to commute to Worthing for a week's run.

In many ways the Connaught was like a finishing school: after drama academy, actors would get their first experience in one of the smaller reps around the country and then, if they were lucky, graduate to the Connaught where any rough edges would be smoothed off and they were ready to rise up the ladder. The very fortunate

Malcolm Farquhar, Martin Friend (seated), Anne Berry and Timothy West in The Leader of the House *(May 1960)*

On Monday Next *is Philip King's farce about life in a tatty weekly rep. With Roland Curram (bandaged head) as the director are Patricia Routledge, Gerald Flood, Angela Browne, John Gorrie, Nicholas Stevenson, Freda Knorr and Pamela Charles*

ones might avoid the smaller rep if they were spotted by Gillam in one of the drama school 'showcases' or if they were recommended to him by a good agent. Al Parker, one of the leading agents of the day, had great faith in Gillam: he and his actress wife, Margaret Johnston, would be at the Connaught virtually every Saturday. When he spotted what he thought was a potential star, like Susannah York, for instance, he would recommend them to the Connaught. A leading film director, Sydney Box, often suggested young players to Gillam. Gillam liked to watch student groups perform: it was as a result of seeing the Cambridge Footlights revue at the Lyric, Hammersmith, that he gave Daniel Massey his professional start.

In 1956 the company was formidable: on stage were Ian Hendry, Roland Curram, Peter Byrne, Peggy Sinclair, Michael Bryant, Daniel Massey, Elizabeth Spriggs, Patricia Routledge, Ian Holm, Keith Baxter and Vanda Godsell. The directors during that year included Jack Williams, Peter Wood, Guy Verney (now freelancing) and Alan Bridges. Disley Jones had left but his assistant, Michael Eve, had been promoted and was doing most of the sets. On the prompt book was Alan Ayckbourn.

Guest artistes included Elizabeth Allen, Sonnie Hale and Henry Kendall. The company always welcomed the arrival of star performers. 'They were so generous in their advice,' recalled Daniel Massey, 'you could learn so much from them.'

As in most schools an 'old boy' network flourished: since directors and company members knew each other's capabilities and strengths, as they moved upwards they would frequently recommend former colleagues for jobs. When Peter Wood became resident director of the Arts Theatre he cast several of the Connaught company in plays there.

1956 saw only ten premieres but most were by the country's leading playwrights including Lesley Storm, Harold Brooke and Kay Bannerman, Sonnie Hale, Robin Maugham and Mary Hayley Bell. Noel Coward wrote two songs for the Connaught

Graham Payn led a cast of 28 in the 1958 production of The Teahouse of the August Moon. *The five sets were designed by Robert Weaver*

production of Hayley Bell's *Treble Key.*

All the company wanted to be in new plays: they loved the opportunity to breathe life into a role which nobody else had played. 'I was very disappointed to find my name was not on the list when the casting for *The Family Tree* went up,' said Roland Curram, even though he had been in most of the other premieres. 'Gillie was always very good,' he continued, 'he made sure that each member of the company got their turn to "shine" every four or five weeks.'

A drunken,moustachioed Ian Holm is carried by Peter Byrne and guest player Barry Sinclair in Something About a Sailor

If the role was particularly long or difficult there was a little bonus in the weekly pay packet: Constance Wake never forgot the £2 extra she got for playing Blanche du Bois in *A Streetcar Named Desire*. When the leading man in *Any Other Business* collapsed on the opening night David Baron, who was playing a supporting role in the production, took over at very short notice. After the final performance Gillie walked into his dressing room, thanked him warmly and slipped him a ten-bob note - David Baron became better known as a playwright under his real name, Harold Pinter.

Gillam was open to suggestions for productions from his directors. Peter Wood desperately wanted to direct Anouilh's *Time Remembered.* Gillam agreed and was rewarded with one of the most magical productions that the Connaught had ever seen.

A constant stream of young players joined the more familiar faces in the company; some didn't stay long but many of them became well known, such as Prunella Scales, Glenda Jackson, Timothy West, Lynn Redgrave, Nicola Pagett, Judy Cornwell, James Fox, Alan Howard, Judy Parfitt, James Bolam, Derek Fowlds, Christopher Timothy and John Merivale. Noel Coward's companion, Graham Payn, had

Beryl Reid, until then better known as a radio comedienne, in one of her roles as an actress. She appeared in Witch Errant *with John Gorrie and Gerald Flood in 1958*

Noel Coward was a frequent visitor to the Connaught. He is seen here with West End impresario Jack Waller and Peggy Mount. Richard Coleman is in the background

played the leading roles in many London musicals and revues but felt he needed more experience in straight roles and asked Gillam to let him join the Worthing company for a few months; but, as one of his colleagues remarked, even the Connaught failed to turn him into an actor.

Directors, nothing more than a name on the programme to many provincial playgoers, included Clifford Williams, Robert Chetwyn, John Schlesinger (whose many film credits include the Oscar-winning *Midnight Cowboy*) and, for one production, Peter Hall. Designers, apart from Disley Jones and Michael Eve, who became known far beyond Worthing, included Hutchinson Scott, Robert Weaver and Kenneth Turner.

Among the many guest artistes who played at the Connaught while at the peak of their fame were Clive Brook, Fay Compton, Jack Buchanan, Renee Ascherson, Jean Kent, Flora Robson, Derek Bond, Joyce Carey, Guy Rolfe, Bill Owen, Frankie Howerd, Millicent Martin, Faith Brook, Naunton Wayne, Dandy Nichols, Irene Handl and Tessie O'Shea, while Glynis Johns flew from America to do one production. When Beryl Reid made her debut at the Connaught she was a highly acclaimed variety and broadcasting comedienne, best known for her impersonation of a revolting Birmingham school child, Monica. Playing straight roles at Worthing (and later Windsor) led to her becoming an outstanding actress.

It was not only on stage that the celebrities were to be seen: many recognisable faces appeared in the stalls. Henry Sherek, the burly impresario and television personality, was a regular visitor, as were Katie Boyle, Gilbert Harding and writer and wit Alan Melville. Interval drinkers could rub shoulders with Jack Buchanan, Graham Greene or Coral Browne. Anna Massey came to support her brother Daniel,

Sir Winston and Lady Churchill arriving at the Connaught in October 1958, to see their daughter, Sarah, in Variations on a Theme

John Clements and his wife, Kay Hammond, would look in to see her son, John Standing, and many other notable actors dropped in to see friends at work. Hollywood celebrities such as Gloria Swanson, Tyrone Power, James Mason, Gladys Cooper and Constance Bennett all saw productions at the Connaught when they were in England.

Although not recognisable to the average patron, the leading London critics were frequently in on opening nights - the amount of publicity that the Connaught obtained for Worthing must have been worth a fortune: this, at least, was recognised by the Borough Council when, in 1959, it invited the Board and the company to drinks at the Town Hall.

Guy Vaesen, the resident director of the Connaught for six years, with Sarah Churchill, who starred in his production of Variations on a Theme

Noel Coward became a regular visitor. In the bar, after the final performance of his *Quadrille*, the leading players, Charles Morgan and Ann Castle quaked as the Master walked towards them. 'Darlings,' he said, 'I wrote this play for Alfred Lunt and Lynn Fontanne - tonight I didn't miss either of them.'

The most memorable night for the Connaught was Friday,

10 October 1958. As soon as it became known that Sarah Churchill was to appear in Worthing after living in America for many years, everyone wanted to know if the war-time leader would be coming to see his daughter act. The management kept a low profile, but the press and television got hold of the news on the day of the visit. Before the performance was due to start more than two thousand people lined Union Place to see Sir Winston and Lady Churchill arrive.

Before the date of Sir Winston's visit was fixed Gillam had already decided to run the production for a fortnight. This meant that he was able to order the scene designer, Robert Weaver, and his assistant to repaint the dressing rooms and corridor through which the great man would walk - a handle was even put on a door which had been without one since nobody could remember when! Even so, this did not stop some sections of the press referring to Sarah's return to the British stage as an appearance with a 'tatty rep' - which it certainly was not.

That production, Rattigan's *Variations on a Theme*, met problems. Sarah Churchill had a reputation for hitting the bottle but during rehearsals and on the first night she behaved magnificently. On the second night, however, Susannah York, in only her ninth week as a professional actress, wondered why the pace of the performance had slowed almost to a stop and why Sarah seemed unable to get her lines out: she was back on the booze. She did, however, remain sober for her father's visit.

This was one of the productions directed by Guy Vaesen, who was appointed resident director in April 1957. He timed his arrival well - just days later the Chancellor of the Exchequer announced the abolition of the crippling Entertainment Tax which was a godsend to theatres, particularly repertory houses like the Connaught who could now plough more back into productions.

In the spring of 1957 Gillam staged Lillian Hellman's famous drama, *The Little Foxes*, but during the preceding week the Connaught saw her lesser known prequel, *Another Part of the Forest,* set in the same house in Alabama in 1888, twelve years earlier than the better known sister piece. Four of the characters appear in both plays, other members of the company had the more difficult task of playing different characters in the second week.

There was one disappointment for Gillam that year. Always fascinated by musical theatre he had suggested to Noel Coward the idea of writing a score for his early play, *The Young Idea.* Coward was interested and plans were made for a production to the extent that Daniel and Anna Massey were fixed to play the two leads. Unfortunately, before Coward got round to composing the music the careers of both Daniel and Anna had taken off and the production never materialised.

Worthing did have a small interest in another musical, however. Early in 1958 Pamela Charles, who had for some months been the company's leading lady, left the Connaught to take over from Sally Ann Howes as Eliza in the Broadway production of *My Fair Lady.* Later, when the show toured Australia, the roles of Henry Higgins and Col. Pickering were played by two of Worthing's stalwarts, Robin Bailey and Kenneth Laird.

Harold Fielding had moved into management, mainly on the musical side, and in 1958 he decided to put on a season of three Agatha Christie plays in repertoire at the Playhouse in Llandudno. Gillam and C.T. (Productions) Ltd. joined in as co-producers and, in effect, a separate Connaught company, including Worthing favourites Elizabeth Spriggs, Peter Byrne and Marjorie Wilde, spent the summer on the North Wales coast.

Everything was done at the Connaught, the sets were built in the workshop and the plays were directed by Guy Vaesen, who would spend Tuesday and Wednesday morning rehearsing the Worthing company and travel up to Llandudno at lunchtime, leaving the evening and all day Thursday to work to work with the Welsh company - 'bear in mind they were all Agatha Christies, we certainly didn't touch anything like *St. Joan*!' In his absence the respective stage managers were in command.

The seasons were repeated in future years bringing in substantial sums to Worthing.

If things were going well in Worthing by now it was a different story in other parts of the country. Weekly repertory was dying. The Stage Year Book for 1956 reported that whereas there had been 138 reps in 1952, the number had now almost halved to 73. Since those figures had been published audiences were dropping still further: even the older, better established companies, seemingly the least likely to be affected, were reporting falls of between 5% and 10%. The White Rose Players at Harrogate closed after thirty years and at Derby Playhouse a rescue operation was launched by the largest local business, Rolls Royce. Several companies were now relying on subsidies from the Arts Council.

The face of entertainment was changing everywhere. It was not only the growing popularity of television (many areas now had ITV as well as the BBC) - though this had brought about the death of variety and had closed many halls - but, increasingly, bingo was taking over theatres.

As early as 1955 the start of a revolution had been seen in London with the production of *Waiting for Godot* and the growing activities of Joan Littlewood and her Theatre Workshop at Stratford East. Powerful new American plays like *A View from the Bridge* and *The Crucible* were beginning to change the face of the West End. Early the following year *Look Back in Anger* burst upon the Royal Court.

Gillam was alive to these changes - *Look Back in Anger* was the first of the 'new wave' to be staged at the Connaught in 1957, as soon as it was released to repertory companies. It was a particularly fine production with Roland Curram, Ian Holm and Pamela Charles and Worthing liked it, voting it very high on the list of most popular plays of the year - higher than Agatha Christie's latest, *The Spider's Web.*

A little later, he opened the winter season with *A Taste of Honey,* following two weeks later with Arnold Wesker's *Roots,* directed at Worthing by John Dexter who had staged it at the Royal Court. Harold Pinter came back to play the part of Mick when the Connaught staged his great success, *The Caretaker.*

In 1958 commercial television came to the south. The growth of the medium began not only to reduce audiences but to make it more difficult to get better known actors to take engagements. They preferred to wait by the 'phone for a call for a TV part - no wonder, since the ITV companies were paying a minimum daily rate equivalent to more than a leading player would get for three weeks in rep!

Worthing still seemed immune from the troubles - invariably financial - which were affecting the others. In fact, the Board agreed that the theatre should be reseated and, to allow extra leg room between the rows, reduced the theatre's capacity from 920 to 867.

Still the American managements and writers were keen to have British premieres staged at the Connaught. In 1960 the American hit, *Kind Sir*, featured guest appearances by Vanessa Lee and Peter Graves with music specially composed by Vivian Ellis. The production subsequently toured for twenty weeks.

A few months later Arthur Laurents, best known for writing the book of *West Side Story,* asked Gillam to produce his Broadway hit, *Time of the Cuckoo*. He agreed if

Laurents would find him a star to take the lead. Laurents persuaded Glynis Johns to fly from Hollywood to Worthing to do the show for a week.

At the end of 1961 there was an outstanding revival of *The Corn is Green* with Flora Robson and Brook Williams, son of the author. After two weeks at the Connaught the production moved to Brighton for a further week before touring South Africa.

By now Gillam was not engaging any of the company on a long-term basis: they were employed production by production, some playing perhaps five or six weeks in succession, some appearing in only one play. Repertory as such had ceased, but the audience was totally unaware of the change - so was the local press.

Following the success of the Llandudno seasons, Harold Fielding began to expand his management interests, presenting, in 1960, *The Billy Barnes Revue*: both Gillam and the Connaught studios were credited with much work on the production. Later that year, when he presented *The Gazebo* at the Savoy Theatre it was a co-production with Gillam in a personal capacity.

A couple of years later he took the Connaught production of *How Are You, Johnnie?,* with the unknown Ian McShane and Derek Fowlds, to the Vaudeville Theatre. Unfortunately it was not a success, running only a few weeks. 'It didn't seem to work as well in London as it had in Worthing,' recalled Fowlds. 'I don't think the changes in the people playing supporting roles helped it.'

Early in 1962, *Theatre World* published an article on Sussex theatres under the depressing title 'The Dwindling Provinces'. Ronald Hill wrote: '(At) the most notable company in Sussex..., the Connaught Theatre in Worthing, plays are, with certain exceptions, produced weekly and their selection is by no means run-of-the-mill fare. Melville Gillam, the brain behind the Connaught, panders to no one section of his audience. He will present Coward, Shakespeare and Delaney in successive weeks, as well as a high proportion of new plays annually.... The Connaught, one observes with admiration, is alive, alert and completely lacking in middle-aged torpor. It is ineligible for any grants and more's the pity in view of its consistently enterprising experimental work.'

Only a few weeks after that article appeared Sarah Miles returned to Worthing to play *St. Joan* - in which Nigel Hawthorne had two minor roles. She had made her professional debut at the Connaught the previous year and was rocketed to fame when she was cast opposite Sir Laurence Olivier in the film *Term of Trial.* That she elected to return to repertory after such a success was applauded in a leader in *The Daily Express.* Talking later to Holly Hill, author of the book *Playing Joan,* Miles revealed that she found the production in Worthing with only one week's rehearsal far more satisfying than the production she subsequently did in Los Angeles.

That July, when the Chichester Festival Theatre opened its doors for the first time under the direction of Sir Laurence, seven members of the company had come from the Connaught.

At the same time the Board was giving thought to increasing income from an external source; the Connaught owned the vacant plot of land between the old entrance to the Connaught Hall and the shops in Chapel Road. A planning application was submitted to the council to redevelop the site as a shop with offices over, the resulting income helping to subsidise the theatre. The application was turned down as it transpired there were embryo plans to widen Union Place and make it into a main artery, plans which, had they materialised, would have meant the demolition of the theatre's foyer. A planning appeal upheld the objection.

That year also saw a rating re-valuation: the figure proposed for the Connaught was 5% of gross annual receipts, then running at £35,900. On appeal, the Local Valuation Office reduced the percentage, a saving to the theatre in actual rates paid of £400.

1963 got off to a bad start, with a very severe winter which closed the theatre throughout February. Just before the closure J. Baxter Somerville, the managing director of Brighton's Theatre Royal, died. The Royal was then still one of the country's leading provincial touring dates, so a replacement was needed urgently. One of the Royal's Board, Glynn Burnand, also sat on the Board of the Connaught. He put forward Gillam's name and, knowing the reputation the Connaught had built up, his Brighton colleagues asked him to open negotiations. From 12 February 1963 Gillam ran both theatres.

This made things much simpler for Guy Vaesen ('Gillam wasn't an easy man to work alongside and neither was I'), but when he left six months later to be replaced by Malcolm Farquhar there were problems. Gillam decided not only to select the plays but to cast them too - often without having read them. A young actor arriving in Worthing to play a character called 'Leslie' was shattered to find the part was the leading lady. On another occasion Gillam omitted to cast the vital role of Miss Marple in a revival of *Murder at the Vicarage.* The oversight was not realised until the day before rehearsals were due to begin: luckily Marjorie Wilde, who lived locally but had virtually retired, was able to take over - her memory not being what it was, the set and props were littered with little aides-mémoire!

Gillam's working pattern had to change: as he had to be at Brighton on Monday for the Royal's first night, he now spent Saturday at Worthing, sitting in on the run-through of next week's show in the morning and watching the final performance of the current production in the evening.

Although all appeared to be going smoothly at both houses, there was a shortage of new plays coming out of London that were suitable for production at Worthing. The centre of focus in London had shifted. With the arrival of the Royal Shakespeare Company at the Aldwych, the opening of the National Theatre at the Old Vic and the English Stage Company committed to developing new writing at the Royal Court, Shaftesbury Avenue was no longer the major force in the capital's theatre.

Weekly rep could not attempt the foreign plays that were proving so successful in London, the works of Brecht, Ionesco, Becket, the American Edward Albee, or even the new wave of British playwrights bringing along such demanding works as *Sergeant Musgrave's Dance, Armstrong's Last Goodnight* or John Whiting's *The Devils*. All needed two, three or, preferably, four weeks of rehearsal. Writers of the former London-success type of play on which weekly rep relied so heavily were now writing for the new and insatiable TV markets instead of the theatre. The result was a spate of revivals.

The year 1963 at Worthing saw only two premieres, but the appearance of Clive Brook in *The Judge's Story* proved a tonic at the box office. April opened with one of the most ambitious productions Gillam had ever attempted: Elmer Rice's *Dream Girl,* with over thirty characters. Only once before seen in the UK - at Liverpool, directed by Willard Stoker - it was such a complex piece to stage that it opened not on the usual Monday but on Tuesday to allow extra rehearsal time. An innovation that year was the hiring of the theatre to the Worthing Musical Comedy Society for their production of *Oklahoma*, the first time that amateurs had been seen at the Connaught since the war.

Although London was no longer so interested in the type of new play that the Connaught had been staging, there were seven premieres in 1964, one of which, ironically, became the biggest hit since *Sailor Beware*, ten years earlier. *Big Bad Mouse* was by the same authors, Philip King and Falkland Cary. Its production brought several managements down from London to see it, and some actors, including Ian Carmichael - even Kenneth Williams returned to see the play, despite his contempt for Worthing. Margot Boyd, who later became the voice of Marjorie Antrobus in the Radio 4 soap, *The Archers,* remembered the excitement of the interest of so many stars. 'We came to meet them all,' she recalled. Eventually it was the comedian Jimmy Edwards, who also saw *Big Bad Mouse* at the Connaught who, with Eric Sykes, turned it into the commercial hit of the 1960s. The way the two comedians played (and ad-libbed) it, however, hugely successful though it was, bore little resemblance to the play as seen at the Connaught.

Philip King was a prolific writer and after *Serious Charge* and *Sailor Beware* most of his plays were premiered in Worthing. Several years earlier he had written to Gillam: 'After my dreadful experience with *Rock-a-Bye* and to a slightly less degree with *Pool's Paradise* I was rapidly losing my faith in the theatre. I know of no worse experience than to sit at rehearsals watching your plays butchered and re-written by alleged 'stars' who don't happen to 'feel' a certain line. I have vowed that any future plays I write will be submitted to Worthing, where, if accepted, I know they will get a proper production and my dialogue will be given its proper chance.'

Despite all the other changes which had taken place in theatre one thing remained unaltered: inexperienced assistant stage managers, the lowest form of life in the entertainment world, were paid peanuts. When Simon Williams came into the profession in 1964 Gillam paid him £1 a week! Although his father, the actor and writer Hugh Williams, did not want his son to go into theatre, he subsidised him to the tune of £8 a week. Was it guilt that led Gillam to stage three of the father's plays while the son was at the Connaught?

For the pantomime, Gillam cast young Williams as the Genie in *Aladdin* at £20 a week. After the four-week run it was back to prompting at £1 a week!

Williams remembered that although BBC 2 was now available on television, and despite the number of revivals the Connaught was forced to stage, business was still good and the leading agents still flocked to the theatre on Saturday evenings when they knew Gillam would be around.

One production Williams remembered was Willard Stoker's revival of the modern dress version of *The Rivals* which he had staged for Birmingham (and the London Festival of Repertory) in 1946. Nigel Hawthorne had returned to Worthing for a second short stint and Jean Kent was engaged to play Mrs. Malaprop. The production, he recalled, was very clever despite Kent trying first to correct all the malapropisms and then deciding to play the role with an American accent.

In addition to *The Rivals* there 23 other revivals in 1965, just one premiere and two touring productions, one with Anna Neagle and the other starring Cicely Courtneidge. In September, to celebrate the thirtieth anniversary of the theatre's opening Edward Knoblock's *Milestones* was given a lavish production (Knoblock had lived in Worthing's imposing Beach House on the seafront). Then, suddenly, audiences began to dwindle and losses grow.

In 1966 the revivals continued as did the decline in audiences, settling that winter at around 2,500 a week, 36% of capacity. It was becoming impossible to continue weekly rep. Although standards were still high, apart from the difficulty of finding plays to stage, actors were no longer prepared to go through the demanding treadmill. Most repertories were rehearsing for a minimum of two weeks and many of them were playing for a fortnight, too. The Arts Council was subsidising more and more companies but it would not contemplate a grant for weekly repertory.

Gillam knew that the only answer was to follow the others and become a fortnightly house. The Board was approached but they laid the blame on the downturn entirely on Gillam who, they said, was paying too much attention to Brighton at Worthing's expense. In the view of the Board the cost of going over to fortnightly productions would be exorbitant and they were not prepared to finance it.

The only alternative was to put the Connaught on the market, and Gillam was authorised to open negotiations with the Borough Council to see if they were interested in taking over. Most of Gillam's meeting were with John Coates, the town's Director of Entertainments. Coates supported the idea and, through his offices, the Council was to discuss the proposition at its meeting on 13 April 1966. As the meeting commenced, John Coates collapsed and was rushed to hospital where he died shortly afterwards. The council continued the debate, deciding to set up a sub-committee to investigate the possible purchase of the theatre.

Two months later no recommendation had been made by the sub-committee and on 15 June Gillam called together the thirty staff and told them that the theatre could not keep going. He spoke to the press. 'Repertory once a week is finished,' he told them. 'We are the last of the weeklies. The commercial theatre does not supply us with sufficient good plays as a weekly. We cannot afford to do a change-over to a fortnightly repertory and put on the type of play which young people are demanding. It is a great turmoil and risk while the change comes into being. Our losses would be enormous. You could not indemnify your shareholders for that time, which may be from six months to a year.

'Only one dividend - in the third year - has been paid. Every penny has gone back into the theatre, in productions and employees' salaries. I think it is sad that Worthing cannot go fortnightly because here is a set-up ready-made for the Corporation. It would be nice if the Corporation took the theatre. Worthing repertory theatre is known internationally.'

The curtain came down on 2 July 1966. There were no parties, even though several former members of the company were in the audience, but a programme note summed it all up: 'We say goodbye with deep regret but without apology. We are proud of the contribution we have made both to local entertainment and to the life of the British Theatre.'

The safety curtain was lowered, the lights turned off and the doors locked. After thirty-four years weekly rep in Worthing was dead.

So what was weekly repertory really like? Undoubtedly summer season, end-of-the-pier reps were pretty awful, but year-round houses run by men (and women) who had flair and who loved theatre, places like Folkestone, Bournemouth and Worthing, achieved a consistently high standard.

Thirty years after its demise Moray Watson looked back. 'Many young actors today are dismissive of weekly repertory work: they cannot imagine that the productions and performances could have been anything other than skin deep and superficial. I often wish that I could take them back in time and watch some fine productions and performances that were accomplished in just one week.

'I do think it's sad that actors today do not have the opportunity to play whole seasons after they leave drama school.

'I was lucky enough to do a whole year of weekly rep at Nottingham and Whitley Bay then a year in fortnightly at Leatherhead and Canterbury and then a year of three weeks at Liverpool.

'Soon after leaving Liverpool I was invited to do two plays for Gillie at Worthing. The first was the premiere of a play by Kieran Tunney called *Royal Exit*. I played King Ferdinand of Bratislava.

'The following week, in total contrast, I played the Brian Rix part (Gregory) in *Reluctant Heroes* by Colin Morris. I've never had so much fun (or heard so much laughter) before or since. They were both directed by Jack Williams who knew exactly what could be accomplished in a week: I felt completely confident working with him.'

Warren Mitchell worked at Worthing only five times but his wife, Constance Wake, was leading lady with the company for eighteen months before moving on to Liverpool and whenever his own engagements permitted he watched her performances. 'Repertory', he said, 'worked on the principal of Parkinson's law: if you have three weeks of rehearsal to get to perfection the company will stretch the time accordingly, if you have only one week to get there you will compress the work into that time. The weekly shows I saw at Worthing were every bit as good as the three-weeklies at Liverpool.'

CHAPTER EIGHT

Directly the Connaught had gone dark campaigners began work to save it. The first on the scene was a long-time supporter of the theatre, 66-year-old Annette Maby, who, with a young enthusiast, David Sulkin, then just seventeen, formed the Preservation of the Connaught Theatre Society.

It was known that the Borough Council was interested in buying the freehold, if not for the theatre at least for its site value, but the Connaught's Board was asking more then the local authority was prepared to pay. The first aim of the Preservation Society was to raise the balance, enable to council to buy the Connaught and then make sure it survived as a theatre. Miss Maby and her sister, Pauline, provided the funds to print posters, car stickers, petition forms and to hire halls for public meetings and fund-raising events.

The young Sulkin believed that fighting would save the theatre, his older partner was sure that justice would prevail. She wrote numerous obsequious letters to influential people in the theatre and had strong support from Bill Fraser, Elsie Randolph, Sybil Thorndike, her husband Sir Lewis Casson, and many others. Neither of them realised that only politics would save the theatre.

It was at this point that representatives of several amateur drama societies decided to take a stand. Describing the Preservation Society as a combination of a young whippersnapper and a dotty old fool, they started a Save the Connaught Campaign.

The committee appointed by the new Campaign had direct access to councillors and soon they took the initiative. By now young David had left Worthing to go to drama school. There was no alternative to the Preservation Society becoming absorbed by the new organisation.

Pauline Maby returned the funds to the original donors where possible, the balance being passed to the treasurer of the Save the Connaught Society.

While all this was going on in the open the Borough Council's sub-committee was trying to agree a price with the vendors. Eventually, at the end of July, a compromise formula was put to the Connaught's Board and a fortnight later the sale was agreed in principle.

Next came negotiations with the Arts Council to see what assistance it would give to keep the Connaught alive; by chance, at that moment central government increased the Arts Council's funding by £1.8 million to £5.7 million.

The Arts Council readily agreed to support the Connaught as a repertory theatre on their usual terms: the theatre, whose productions must run for a minimum of two weeks, could not be directly controlled by Worthing Borough Council. A separate, non-profitmaking distributing trust company would have to be set up which would elect a Board of Governors to control the theatre. The Board was to consist of twelve members, six nominated by the Trustees, the other half to be appointed by the Council but of these not more than five could be sitting members.

Despite the Arts Council's attempts to avoid local authority control of its clients, Worthing Borough Council maintained an iron grip on the Connaught. The chairman of the 'independent' Board of Governors was always a councillor, its secretary and treasurer always council officers.

A deal that was then almost unique was achieved: the Arts Council would give a grant of £8,000 to keep the theatre functioning and the local authority would provide a similar amount. Later such parity funding became a prerequisite for all Arts Council regional theatre funding.

The proposals for the purchase and running, having passed through various committee stages, were put before the full council on 5 October 1966, together with a 4,000-signature petition to save the theatre.

Some councillors had doubts: for the past three years the pier summer shows had lost money, and a week's season of three Agatha Christie plays staged there a month earlier had drawn an audience of 2,422 - roughly the same as the Connaught had been getting in its dying stages. Was it worthwhile risking more of the ratepayers' money, they asked?

Councillors supporting the Connaught argued that the plans should be given a try, promising that if, after two years, the venture was not a success, the theatre should be closed and its future reconsidered. Whatever happened it was guaranteed that the council's annual subsidy would never exceed £8,000. The proposition was carried by 23 votes to 11.

At this time the country was in the grip of a financial squeeze and a memorandum on public spending had just been received from the Ministry of Housing and Local Government which imposed severe restrictions on spending for amenity, cultural, leisure and educational projects. Whilst this did not have any bearing on the purchase of the Connaught, it did restrict the amount that could be spent on any subsequent alterations. Councils which have since acquired theatres have, almost invariably, employed specialist architects to undertake modernisation and refurbishment. Had this course been open to Worthing at that time it might have proved far more economic than the unending re-jigging which started in 1966.

The object had been achieved: the Connaught was saved and before long the theatregoers of Worthing, few though they might be, would be enjoying their pastime again. Little did they know what was in store for them!

The Worthing and District Connaught Theatre Ltd was soon formed and by the end of January 1967 the Board of Governors had been appointed. In addition to five councillors, the local authority nominated to the sixth place a local resident, Dennis Morris, who was about to retire as head of BBC Light Entertainment. The Trustees, who were representatives of over fifty societies, businesses and other local authorities in West Sussex, appointed to the Board Leslie Evershed Martin, founder of the Chichester Festival Theatre, Dr Walter Eysslinck, director of the Arts Centre of the University of Sussex, and local playwright Constance Cox, plus three others. Of the twelve Governors only one third had any experience of the provision of professional entertainment.

The post of Artistic Director was advertised and in April, from the 127 applications received, the post went to Christopher Denys. Aged thirty, he was an Associate Director of the Bristol Old Vic where, for the past two years, he had been responsible for the successful running of the Bristol Little Theatre, forerunner of the Bristol Old Vic Studio.

From his arrival in June 1967, he threw himself into organising the theatre alterations, engaging the company, planning the season and, above all, promoting the Connaught throughout West Sussex. He was enthusiastically joined in this by the new General Manager, Michael Freeman, who was just two years younger than his colleague. Within a fortnight of their arrival the opening date was fixed for 5th September.

The sixties were the decade of youth: the Beatles reigned supreme. Melville Gillam, 25 years older than his successor, knew this - one of the reasons he had given for the Connaught's closure was that weekly repertory could not put on the type of play which young people were demanding.

In his first press statement Chris Denys outlined his policy. The plays would be the best that were available, ranging from the classics to the avant-garde and experimental work. His aim was to provide a theatre for every member of the West Sussex community, especially the young. There would be 'open days' at the theatre where students could spend the morning watching the company rehearse, meet the technicians, go backstage, then see a performance in the afternoon. Additionally, the company would be paying regular visits to schools. The Arts Council had made additional funds available for youth work and a van and portable stage had been ordered. As for the plays, 'When I announce the first plays,' Denys said, 'we may see a few raised eyebrows because I am not going to give people the plays they are expecting. I want to surprise them.'

In the event he did not so much surprise as astonish.

CHAPTER NINE

Interest was running high. The newly formed Connaught Theatre Club, with Bill Fraser as President, had over eleven hundred members, two hundred of them under nineteen. At a club meeting shortly before the theatre reopened, Fraser revealed that when the theatre closed in 1940 he had kept the key of the stage door as a memento: handing it over to Chris Denys, he said 'The moment has now come when I should return it to the Connaught Theatre.'

Gradually details of the new company began to emerge, and it was apparent that the new director was bringing many of his colleagues from Bristol. Eric Johns, editor of *The Stage,* wrote: 'The Connaught is fortunate in being directed by so young and enthusiastic a man of the theatre as Christopher Denys, who bears the hallmark of the Bristol Old Vic, one of the finest repertory theatres in the world. I hope Worthing residents and visitors realise how lucky they are.'

There is little doubt that the new Connaught, like its predecessors, could have ranked amongst the best of regional repertories in the country, but it was doomed to be scuppered by the very people who had rescued it.

The opening production was to be *The Beggar's Opera* with Barbara Windsor and, in the role of Macheath, Frederick Jaeger, who had been a popular member of Gillam's company and had just completed a long West End run as leading man in *Lock Up Your Daughters.* This was to be followed by Noel Coward's *Private Lives,* starring Adrienne Corri, then would come the astonishment: plays by Max Frisch (who's he? they asked), J.M.Synge, Shakespeare, Ibsen and, in December, *Little Malcolm and His Struggle Against the Eunuchs* - that was a word you didn't often hear in Worthing.

Sixteen weeks and not a sign of Agatha Christie!

The opening night was a gala occasion and all available seats had been sold within twenty-four hours of the box office opening. The remainder - about half- were reserved for guests of the Trust and of the Borough Council. Among the guests were several who had connections with the old Connaught: as well as Gillam himself, there were Dame Flora Robson, Elsie and Doris Waters and the author of *The Blue Lamp,* Lord Ted Willis. Invited but unable to attend were Bill Fraser, Sir Donald Wolfit, Sean Connery and Albert Finney, all of whom sent messages of goodwill. Other messages came from the Rt. Hon. Jennie Lee, MP, Minister for the Arts, Sir Ralph Richardson, Sir Laurence Olivier on behalf of the National Theatre, Sir Michael Redgrave, Sir John Clements and the Chichester Festival Theatre, Dora Bryan, Peter Hall, Frankie Howerd and Val May for the Bristol Old Vic.

The only sour note came from one local councillor who returned his guest tickets for seats in the seventeenth row, complaining that he was not climbing into his dinner jacket just to sit in the pit with the hobble-de-hoys. Little did he realise that he might have felt safer there than in the front where, amongst the honoured guests, there was a party which included Barbara Windsor's then husband, Ronnie Knight and his friends, whose names tended to appear more frequently on the crime pages than the arts pages of the nation's press.

During its closure many alterations had been made to the theatre. In the foyer new sales counters had been installed for retailing confectionery, books and magazines.

Upstairs the bar had been adapted so that it could also serve as a restaurant. Another small bar had been had been created at the back of the stalls and there were coffee counters at both sides of the auditorium, hidden by curtains during the performance.

The biggest alterations were the extension of the stage into the auditorium, reducing seating capacity to 710, and the building of a false ceiling hiding the ornately painted dome which had always been a feature of the theatre. All this was forgiven by the traditionalists, but they were aghast to find that the whole of the auditorium had been painted black.

The first night, however, was a triumph: at the final curtain the company was greeted with cheers and bouquets. That Saturday evening every seat was sold but no trace could be found of the 'House Full' board.

Although the opening production was a success both artistically and financially (it grossed over £3,500 in its three-week run), it soon became clear that the reopened Connaught was not at all what the campaigners had battled for. They had expected a return to the elegance of the silk purse they had been used to but, instead, they felt they had been given a pig's ear.

The complaints came loud and long: they didn't like the absence of the National Anthem, the house manager was not in a dinner jacket to greet them, out had gone the smartly dressed audience to be replaced by sweaty jeans, the once elegant bar had become a caff (and there were complaints about the coffee), the actors were too young (the fact that their past favourites, such Richard Coleman and Susannah York, had come to Worthing straight from drama school was conveniently forgotten), they didn't like the all black auditorium ('Just like a funeral parlour,' declared one disgruntled patron) and they certainly were not going to like the plays.

The men's chorus in The Beggar's Opera, *the re-opening production directed by Christopher Denys in September 1967*

Eleanor Bron (left) with Chris Harris and John White in Playboy of the Western World, *directed by Christopher Denys in 1967 with sets by Catherine Browne*

The only thing they didn't seem to object to was that there was now no charge for the programmes.

Soon the school tours were under way and on Sunday evenings the theatre was open for a mixed programme of jazz, chamber music, poetry readings, talks and discussions.

Certainly the new management had aimed for a different audience and they responded, whatever the old brigade might think. Although the third production, Max Frisch's *Andorra,* did not do well in its first week, the youngsters poured in for the second. *The Playboy of the Western World* played to over 60% capacity and Eleanor Bron's outstanding performance in *Hedda Gabler* was appreciated by large audiences. The eunuch play was poorly supported, but in those days the two weeks prior to Christmas were traditionally bad for theatres.

Meanwhile the Borough Council had another entertainment problem: the thirteen-week season of the *Fol-de-Rols* at the pier had made a loss of over £8,000. It was the policy to engage managements for the summer show on a three-year basis and this was the time when the *Fol-de-Rols* contract expired. A change was decided on for 1968: the council would engage a producer and run the show themselves at an estimated cost of £1,400 - a decision which was to play havoc with the Connaught's fortunes at a later date.

This Christmas the pier also had a bearing on the Connaught's plans. The previous year, with the theatre closed, the council had engaged a management to stage

The 1968 production of Tom Taylor's Victorian melodrama, The Ticket of Leave Man, *staged by Christopher Denys and designed by Catherine Browne*

pantomime at the pier and since contracts for the current year had to be negotiated before it was known whether the Connaught would be back in action, *Dick Whittington* had been booked. With this in mind Chris Denys decided to back a winner by opening *Charley's Aunt* for a four-week run on Boxing Day.

The production gave Chris Harris, now one of the most successful pantomime 'dames' in the business, his first chance to appear in drag as Lord Fancourt Babberly, Charley's Aunt. When Claire Sutcliffe had to relinquish the part of Ela at short notice during the run, the young Gwyneth Powell stepped into her first major role: before long she had become one of the Connaught's major assets, even having the leading role in a new musical written specially for her. Another young member of the company at that time, Marcus Plantin, was destined to take a very different route: he became Network Director of Independent Television.

Despite the whinges, the standards set by Chris Denys were very high. 1968 opened with a spectacular revival of an old Victorian melodrama, *The Ticket of Leave Man,* followed by a totally enthralling *Waiting for Godot*; then came *The Glass Menagerie*, featuring Bessie Love and Francesca Annis which, after its fortnight in Worthing, toured to several major cities. The final play of the first financial year was Shakespeare's *Richard III,* with Frederick Jaeger in the title role.

During the seven months since reopening there had been twelve productions which had produced a box office income of £24,952 and, despite the heavy costs of setting up the new company, a net surplus of £114.

But there were other storms to be weathered. Whilst Shakespeare's version of *Richard III* was earning plaudits in the theatre, a modern parallel written by Chris Denys and toured to schools was bringing thunderous noises from the traditionalists. It was a travesty of Shakespeare, left-wing claptrap, they declared. Letters of protest occupied columns of the local press. So great was the clamour that

Christopher Denys threw new light on Edward Albee's famous Who's Afraid of Virginia Woolf? *by casting two black players, Thomas Baptiste and Isabelle Lucas, in the leading roles with Alice Fraser and Colin Fisher as their young neighbours*

the play was staged at the Connaught one Sunday evening followed by a discussion on its merits. A full house gave it overwhelming backing.

The other continuing complaint was, of course, the choice of plays - too much culture, not enough entertainment. In reality it was a period of excitement, Chris Denys was doing what he set out to do: surprise. If those who had enjoyed *When We Are Married* had ventured to the two plays which followed, *Sergeant Musgrave's Dance* and *The Country Wife,* they would have appreciated not only the excellence of the casting but the ingenuity of the technical staff in achieving such a uniformly high standard in three very different productions.

The sniping continued, however, coming from a very small but a very vocal minority, many, it seems, prominent in the Theatre Club (of which Chris Denys was a committee member) who also had the ear of the local press. The Arts Council, on the other hand, was impressed with the programme at the Connaught and its involvement with the schools.

The Board, too, was supportive. Early in 1968, the chairman, Alderman Frank Kenton, stated: 'One or two of the plays in the Autumn season gave rise to a certain amount of criticism and discussion but this is surely a good thing. If we are to have a 'live' theatre we must try to cater for all tastes and this inevitably means entering the controversial as well as the 'cosy' fields.

'Thinking back over the black period when the theatre was closed and the hopes which many of us had for the future, I think it is true to say that the new theatre is proving a success and our thanks are due to Christopher Denys, his staff and the performers for all their efforts and to the public for the support they have given this venture.

'Now the honeymoon may be coming to an end and it is up to us all - management and public alike - to see that the 'marriage' settles down to become a long and happy one. By all means let us have comment and criticism - as long as it is constructive - for in this way we shall at least know that what we are doing is worthy of comment and, we hope, continued support.'

But if there was disquiet, audiences were coming, once again, from as far afield as Portsmouth, Horsham, Brighton and beyond.

On Sunday, 7 April 1968, the Connaught staged an old-time music hall. Along with the resident players, Gwyneth Powell, Michael Mackenzie and Reginald Long, the guest 'turns' were Sandy Powell and Bill Fraser, making his first appearance on the Connaught stage for nineteen years.

An old friend from Gillam's day was also featured: Gil Roberts, who had been playing the piano interludes and conducting the pantomime orchestra a few years back, provided the music for the show and at Christmas he was back in the pit for Connaught pantomime once more.

With the coming of the summer months lighter fare was provided with a musical, revivals of *See How They Run* and *Hay Fever;* the resident company even did a week of Edwardian Music Hall. The autumn saw, as in the days of the Overture Players, the return of 'meatier' works. An ebullient *Twelfth Night* was followed by Brendan Behan's *The Hostage,* then came *She Stoops to Conquer,* the very fine Russian three-hander, *The Promise* and, finally, *Who's Afraid of Virginia Woolf?* with two black actors in the leading roles.

Robinson Crusoe was a type of pantomime that Worthing was not used to. Written and directed by Chris Denys, it was aimed to appeal very much more to young children than to adults. Despite another barrage of letters of complaint to the press, it was seen by over 20,000 people and took £6,500 at the box office.

One new aspect of the Connaught was that, since it was no longer a private venture, the comings and goings of senior staff became public knowledge and with it came speculation over departures. Who couldn't get on with who? Who was creating trouble? In most cases people probably left for quite ordinary reasons, such as better jobs or just wanting a change. Whereas in the past it was the performers who caught the headlines, now it was the technicians.

The General Manager, Michael Freeman, had left almost as soon as the theatre had reopened and early in 1969 the designer, Catherine Browne, who had come from Bristol with Chris Denys, resigned. Of all the staff changes possibly the most significant was the arrival of Robert English. Coming on an Arts Council bursary, at the end of a six-month study period he was taken on to the staff as Resident Associate Director, to cause, before long, as big a furore as the Connaught had ever seen.

Life in a subsidised rep was very different from the old 'weekly' days, particularly backstage. No longer did designers spend hours painting the sets, this was now the work of a specialist crew. There was also a wardrobe department to provide all the costumes, whether period or modern - no longer did the cast (whatever they were paid) have to provide their own. There was a production manager to compile budgets, oversee all the other departments and ensure that everything came together for the opening night. There were musical directors, lighting supervisors and master carpenters, all with assistants.

In the front of house area there was a general manager, house manager, catering manager, box office manager, accountant and secretary and part-time employees plus usherettes recruited from the Theatre Club. The bar was now open all day, providing not just alcohol and light refreshments but full scale meals at both lunch time and in the evenings.

The biggest change, though, was probably the dress rehearsal, no longer pressed into the few hours before the Monday evening's paying audience arrived but allocated a whole day and a half before curtain up.

Although the load for the artistes had changed it had not lessened. Gwyneth Powell recalled that when she and five other assistant stage managers reported for duty on the first day of rehearsals for the opening production, they were handed paintbrushes and ordered to redecorate the toilets. That done, they were presented with heaps of cotton wool and told to make the wigs for *The Beggar's Opera* - none had a clue where to start. For a while she combined appearing on stage with serving behind the bar whilst one of her colleagues, when not on stage, was the chef! Despite her rising reputation as an actress she remained an assistant stage manager (on the appropriate pay) for nearly a year. After the dress rehearsal for *Portrait of a Queen*, in which she played the lead, she re-set the stage and was told by Chris Denys, 'You leave the theatre this afternoon as assistant stage manager and return this evening as an actress.' Promotion and a pay rise!

Although rehearsal periods were longer, the fully fledged actors found themselves with little time to spare since most were involved in the tours round the schools which took up a considerable part of their day.

The Connaught had been lucky: it had never been in the hands of a grasping commercial manager desperate to make money. Fraser and Bell ploughed back into the productions much of the money they were making, then the J. Arthur Rank Organisation was ready to finance expensive productions and in Gillam's time Bill Chapple had been happy to put his hand in his pocket whenever anything was needed. Now, however, the financiers were the members of the public, the tax and rate-payers, the majority of whom had not the slightest interest in theatre not just in Worthing, but anywhere in the country. Their interests had to be protected.

1969 was not a good year for the Connaught: audiences began to decline and so did standards on the stage. At the end of the second financial year (31 March 1969) the accounts showed a deficit of over £1,500. The income from the box office had been £38,000, catering added another £12,000, the Arts Council grant had risen to £17,149 while the local authority figure remained at £8,000.

It was three months before the figures were made public at the end of July, by which time audiences were declining still further. Following a new musical, *Bakerloo to Paradise* (which, starring Kenny Lynch and Pip Hinton, went on to tour such 'number one' dates as the New Theatre, Hull, the Theatre Royal, Nottingham, and the Birmingham Hippodrome) came two plays of the weekly rep 'style': *Wait Until Dark,* which played to 22% capacity, and *White Cargo,* whose audience dropped to 15% or about 1,575 people over fifteen performances, considerably less than the average attendance during the final weeks of the old rep.

The chairman of the Board admitted the situation was critical and that some drastic move would have to be made if the Connaught was to continue. The

Borough Council came to the rescue by providing up to £1,500 as a guarantee against loss.

The dissenters, however, went into action. In late summer an advertisement appeared in the local press calling for other old patrons to rally again and press for a return to weekly rep, for an improved standard of production, a more widely acceptable choice of plays and three matinee and five evening performances a week.

In interviews with the press the promoters called for a break with the Arts Council and the ending of the school tours. Instead of writing and acting plays for youngsters, both the director and the cast should spend their time improving standards in the theatre itself, said people who admitted that they had not set foot in the Connaught for over a year.

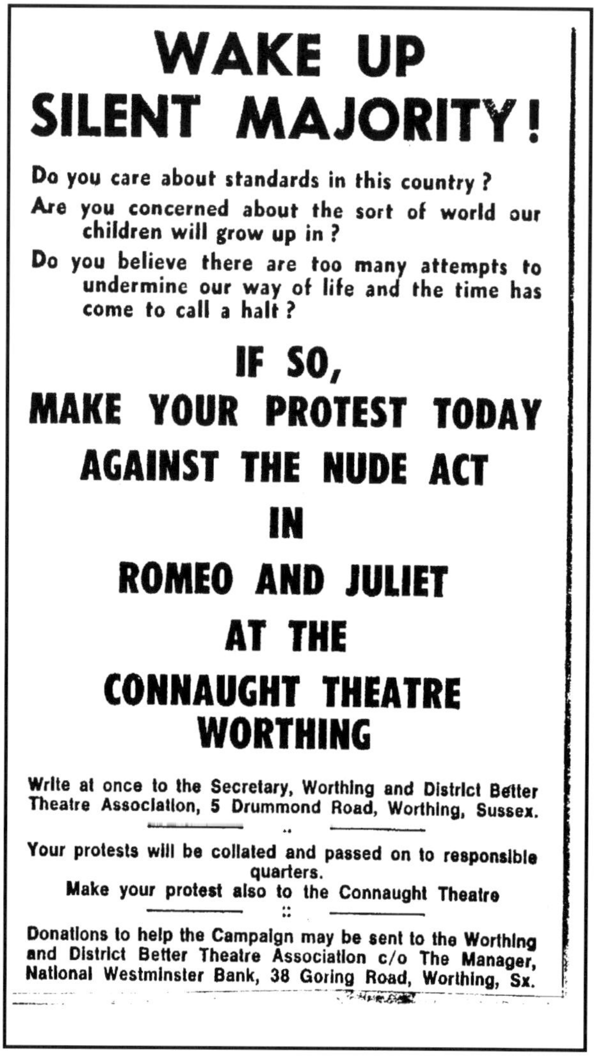

An advertisement which appeared in the local papers in April 1970

The logic in favour of weekly rep was unclear: it had already been revealed how badly *Wait Until Dark* and *White Cargo* had done and as for extra matinees, the usual afternoon attendance currently enjoyed at the theatre was under 40. Eventually the dissent calmed down and audiences did build up during the late summer and autumn. Ironically for the protesters, Chris Denys was invited to Downing Street in January, 1970, to discuss with the Prime Minister, Harold Wilson, and other experts, the future of young people's theatre in Britain.

While the Connaught's problems were being aired that summer the pier was again facing difficulties. The first of the Corporation's own summer shows the previous year had lost money, this year the loss had exceeded the grant to the Connaught. The Entertainments Committee decided to abandon staging its own shows and opened negotiations with Chris Denys for the Connaught to take over the presentation of a summer revue in 1970 with separate funding from the Entertainment budget.

Meanwhile, the Board of the Pitlochry Festival Theatre invited Chris Denys to direct four plays for them. Since there was an Assistant Director who could carry on at Worthing, the Connaught Board agreed to three months' leave of absence for the Scottish trip.

By the start of the fourth financial year the picture was looking rosier. In February the Borough Council had agreed to increase its grant from £8,000 to £24,000, while the Entertainments Committee was putting up another £15,000 for a nine-week summer show. Added to that audiences were increasing again.

Staff changes, however, were still frequent: two more General Managers had come and gone and, almost in desperation, for some while Chris Denys had been combining those duties with his work as Artistic Director.

Whilst Chris Denys was in Scotland a young actress made her professional debut at the Connaught in a production which caused public protest meetings, petitions, untold letters to the local press and both national and international news coverage. Robert English announced that in one scene of his staging of *Romeo and Juliet,* Susan Penhaligon and Michael Mackenzie would appear naked. All hell was let loose!

Depravity, left-wing lunacy and the angels of Satan were all at work in Worthing. The censorship of stage presentations by the Lord Chamberlain had come to an end eighteen months earlier, permitting for the first time productions featuring nudity such as *Hair* and *Oh, Calcutta!*. If any Peeping Toms were lured to the Connaught by the furore they were to be disappointed: the scene was logical, brief and the lighting was very subtle in a generally uninspired production. (Susan Penhaligon's grandmother travelled from Falmouth to see the notorious production and complained later that she was disappointed at not having been able to see more of Romeo!)

In June the first of three editions of *Summertime 70* opened. The resident company was supplemented by some experienced light entertainment performers (Pip Hinton came back again) and the Municipal Orchestra was in the pit. The whole thing was a disaster.

Needless to say the old brigade had plenty of ammunition now with which to attack the running of the theatre and the standard on the stage. The July meeting of the Trustees was highly acrimonious.

Shortly after the debacle Chris Denys announced his resignation. In his official statement he said that he had been invited back to Pitlochry for the 1971 season and he could not expect the Connaught Board to give him leave for a second time. He added that his time in Worthing had been enjoyable if worrying at times. Combining the posts of General Managers and Artistic Director had proved impossible. 'It was,' he said, 'conceit that made me think I could do it.'

Within a week of the resignation being announced his assistant, Robert English, who was on holiday in Spain, wrote to the Board telling them he was not coming back.

Chris Denys left Worthing in February, 1971, just weeks after the arrival of a new General Manager.

CHAPTER TEN

Ronald Jameson was 47 and came to Worthing from being a senior member of the administrative staff at Chichester Festival Theatre. Previous posts had included Joan Littlewood's Theatre Workshop, the Royal Shakespeare Company and the Welsh National Theatre.

He was joined in March by the new Artistic Director, Ted Craig, an Australian who had spent the three previous years running the Crewe Theatre.

In regional theatre a change of director usually meant not only a change of style but also a change of company. The opening productions proved a catholic choice. Molière's *The Miser* was followed by a translation from the Japanese, *Rashomon*, then an Australian play which had first been seen in Gillam's time, *The Summer of the Seventeenth Doll, The Man With a Load of Mischief* and, finally, the popular Frederick Lonsdale comedy, *On Approval*. Both the choice of the new Artistic Director and his selection of plays was considered sufficiently important for the *Daily Telegraph* to give him a quarter-page interview.

Among the company were David Suchet - most impressive in *Rashomon* - and, for a short stay, Gwen Taylor, followed for a longer period by Susan Brown. Another discovery of Ted Craig's was a young man whose first professional job was in the Connaught's Theatre-in-Education team. Asked what his ambition was by the local press, he replied 'to become a director with the Royal Shakespeare Company': Ian Judge now directs for all the major drama and opera companies.

Plans were being formulated for the summer: there was to be no summer show this year and, for the first time, the pier went over to 'one night stands'. Ted Craig

Centre stage is 25 year old David Suchet in the role of Pastor Manders, with Paul Gregory as Oswald and Judy Nunn as Regina in Ibsen's Ghosts, *staged by Ted Craig in May 1971. The set was designed by Stuart Stanley*

planned a repertoire of productions to run from the middle of June until the end of September. There would be something for everyone: Victorian Music Hall, Shaw's *Candida,* a couple of popular favourites, *Dial 'M' for Murder* and *Boeing-Boeing*, finally, the Royal Shakespeare Company's big success, *The Hollow Crown.*

Worthing, like so many other British coastal towns, was now having to rely less and less on holiday visitors; Britons had started going to the Continent while foreign tourists had yet to brave the vagaries of the British climate. Theatres were beginning to depend on residents for the bulk of their summer audiences and Worthing residents did not like repertoire.

At the July meeting of the Trustees the Chairman of the Board told them that throughout the previous year there had been a steady decline in audiences, with the theatre achieving an average capacity of only 27%, about 2,800 patrons at fifteen performances. For the first four months of the current financial year the situation had become even worse and unless it could be remedied at once there was a real possibility that the theatre would close in September. The die-hards went back into action, still wanting a return to weekly repertory and still not getting it.

The repertoire system, however, was brought to an end on 7 August, *Dial 'M' for Murder* now running for an unbroken three weeks, followed by a similar run for *Boeing-Boeing* and then three weeks of Agatha Christie's *The Unexpected Guest* - the first Agatha Christie for five years!

It may not have been weekly rep but it was the same type of entertainment and it brought the audiences back. By September all thought of closing the theatre had vanished. Through the autumn the same type of play was presented, old 'popular' successes - the sequence being broken only by a not very successful production of the rarely performed Russian play *He Who Gets Slapped* which brought back to Worthing an old favourite of Gillam's days, Gerald Flood.

For the run-up to Christmas there was a children's musical for which, as for the pantomime, costumes, sets and props were made by third-year students at the West Sussex College of Design, so reducing overheads dramatically.

Lock Up Your Daughters opened the winter season followed by another Agatha Christie, plays by Neil Simon and Noel Coward and a thriller.

Although not out of the wood, the financial situation was improving.

Throughout 1972 a similar policy of presenting popular plays was pursued (even the Shakespeare was a 'fun' production of *The Comedy of Errors)* and in the summer a three-week run of the musical, *Robert and Elizabeth*, with the then unknown Ruth Madoc in the lead, attracted full houses at almost every performance.

'Just like the old times again,' one patron was heard to remark.

To compensate for the continual run of populist plays in the Connaught itself, Ted Craig tried an experiment in the old Connaught Hall. Used as the theatre workshop (and having been allowed to fall into appalling decay since its purchase by the council) the building was no longer licensed for public performance. However, Craig cleared a space, moved in some chairs and, in March, staged a few performances of Arthur Miller's *The Price* - since the play is set in an overcrowded attic the Hall added atmosphere to the piece. Admission (free) was obtained on purchase of a full-price ticket for *Barefoot in the Park* in the main house. The experiment was repeated in June with Ann Jellicoe's *The Knack.*

Confidence had returned to the Connaught: coach and party bookings were up and the catering side, too, was improving. The Board and the Borough Council felt sufficiently assured of the theatre's future to undertake a complete revamp of the building following the introduction of new safety regulations. During the three weeks of pantomime rehearsals £30,000 was spent on enlarging the stage, repairing the roof, installing new seating and carpeting, creating a new dress circle and fitting pine panels to the walls.

When the Connaught reopened on Boxing Day, 1972, it seemed almost like a completely new theatre. The reduction in seating by 180 to only 530, however, meant an increase in prices.

Just as everything seemed to be going so well Ted Craig sprung an unpleasant surprise: he had been invited to become the associate director of the resident theatre company at the new Sydney Opera House. He would not be renewing his two-year contract when it expired in March.

The search was on for a new Artistic Director.

From 62 applications the post went to Nic Young who, for the past three years, had been Artistic Director of the Ludlow Festival. Prior to that, he had been assistant director on the Oxford University Drama Society's production of Marlowe's *Dr. Faustus* which featured Richard Burton and his wife, Elizabeth Taylor (a production about which *The Times* had been scathing).

His first production, Ustinov's *The Love of Four Colonels*, opened on 3 April 1973, just two days before a new tax was introduced to the country - Value Added Tax. As usual there was a new company but Ted Craig's 'popular' policy continued.

Addressing the Theatre Club, the new director told them that what he intended to provide was not a theatre of the West End type nor a museum to the plays that were popular fifty years before - good, strong theatre was what he was after. He had gone through the figures since the reopening to find out what people in Worthing wanted.

Since, apart from Alan Ayckbourn's successes, there were still few 'commercial' plays coming out of London, there was no alternative to reviving past favourites. No longer were there demands for a return to weekly rep, nor accusations of a bad choice of plays or poor acting: Worthing was content to watch indifferent productions of such old pieces as *Rope, Ladies in Retirement* and *The Little Hut.* Later, more respectable productions of D.H. Lawrence's *The Daughter in Law* and Chekhov's *Uncle Vanya* did enliven the programme, if not the box office for audiences were melting away again, 20% down on the previous year.

Complacency, depression or boredom, perhaps, had hit the Theatre Club as members had drifted away and the total of supporters had fallen to below 400.

The restaurant had been revamped and offered a four-course, candlelit dinner plus a top price seat for £2. At the other extreme, youngsters under 25 could, on Monday nights, get the best seats for only 20p - a similar concession applied to senior citizens at the Wednesday matinee.

1974 opened to another shock when, on 4 January, the General Manager, Ronald Jameson, who had been instrumental in the Connaught's revival, resigned for 'personal reasons'. Although he had given three months' notice he was released at once and his duties were taken over by Town Hall staff for almost six months until the arrival of 28-year-old Liz Pearson. One of fifteen applicants, she had originally trained in stage management at the Bristol Old Vic Theatre School. After six years backstage she trained in theatre administration and, for two years, had been promoting drama for the Renaissance Theatre Trust in the north west.

This was the year of rampant inflation, with the prices of some commodities going up weekly. Both those working at the theatre and the Board realised they had big problems to face. The Council of Repertory Theatres reported that six of its

Nic Young's 1976 production of Joe Orton's outrageous farce, What the Butler Saw, *revealed a lot of Alan Johns, Shirley Stelfox, Clive Wooster and newcomer Marina Sertis. Angela Muhl designed the show*

twenty-six members were facing immediate bankruptcy and all were contemplating serious cutbacks in their programmes.

During the winter audiences dropped to between 30%-36% of capacity (159 to 190 per performance). Most of the plays were 'popular'; they were, on the whole, reasonably well directed and set while the acting, if not outstanding, was adequate, but if they had been produce in a greengrocer's shop they would have to have been classified as 'Class II'. Perhaps Worthing was still 'too close to London, ducky' (or Brighton or Chichester) to get away with that.

When, that summer, the company staged *The Day After the Fair* - which played to the second largest audiences since the Connaught reopened in 1967 - Sally Geeson, who had been one of the younger generation in Sid James's highly successful TV sit-com, *Bless this House,* gave a sparky performance in the crucial role of the maid and shook the resident members of the company into more classy performances than usual.

Unlike previous managers, Nic Young did not appear to attract any special talents until, in 1976, a dynamic young actress with an unusual name, Marina Sertis, galvanised a decidedly lack-lustre production of Joe Orton's *What the Butler Saw.* A shapely and appealing Ophelia in *Hamlet,* she soon vanished from the Connaught, lost to view, it seemed, forever. Ask a devotee of *Star Trek* today about Counsellor Troi and he will tell you everything about her except that she began her career in Worthing - Marina Sertis took the rocket ship to the planets!

The 'true blue' Conservative council was beginning to be attacked by the local Ratepayers Association who now held several seats and began querying the

Connaught's subsidy. Their leader (he who had turned down his seats in the seventeenth row on reopening night) questioned the theatre being run by a separate Trust instead of directly by the council; presumably he was unaware that this would instantly remove the Arts Council's contribution to the theatre.

When the actors union, Equity, negotiated a revised minimum wage for actors of £35, an increase of £15 a week, the Connaught's Board had to look at its programming.

An extra £34,000 a year would be needed to cover the increased wages and production costs. It was decided that, from March 1975, productions, instead of running for a fortnight, would be staged for three weeks, opening on a Wednesday evening with a reduced price preview in the afternoon. Further, the theatre would close for the month of June, staff numbers would be reduced and seat prices would rise above the present average of £1.

In the theatre itself it was decided to try to attract more 'names' to make guest appearances and to improve publicity. Liz Pe arson devoted all her time and effort to promoting the Connaught, giving talks to women's organisations, businessmen's clubs and virtually any other group that would listen. Edward Woodward and the New Era Jazz Band - who had no previous connection with the Connaught - gave their services for a Sunday concert to raise funds for the theatre.

At the same time the school tours were expanded: this was an area which was always - and remains - of importance to Nic Young, and a drive for membership by the Theatre Club increased support to over 500.

An innovation was to stage late night shows on Friday evenings when the company could break new ground with revues and one-act plays: the first was Tom Stoppard's *The Real Inspector Hound* and at first houses were good - but not much money was made with all tickets at 20p each.

At this moment a new problem faced the council: the structure of the Pier Pavilion was deteriorating fast and the building was unlikely to remain sound for very much longer. The question was: should a new theatre be built which might replace not only the pier's pavilion but the Connaught too? It wasn't, of course.

The following year, 1975, as planned, the theatre closed for the month of June during which time the bar and restaurant were redecorated. But two of the three productions prior to this had lost almost £2,500 and both the Board and the Borough Council were worried: the finances were not good, the Connaught had no reserves and although the Arts Council grants had risen each year in line with inflation, the local council's £24,000 had not been increased since 1969 and was now worth only £11,300 in real terms. Seat prices, too, had not increased as much as they should have done.

When the theatre reopened in July, the guest stars began to arrive: Desmond Carrington was seen a couple of times, Cicely Courtneidge struggled valiantly to remember her lines in *Move Over Mrs. Markham* while Christopher Neame and Stacey Dorning were *Romeo and Juliet* (no nude scenes this time). The production of the musical *Man of La Mancha* was a classic example of an artistic success and a financial disaster.

The following year opened with another musical, *Can Can*, with Elizabeth Larner in the lead and the Municipal Orchestra in the pit. Then came a co-production with Ray Cooney Productions and Gee F. Productions of the premiere of *Carry on Jeeves,* a desperately poor piece despite the appearances of Derek Nimmo, Dulcie

Gray and Jack Watling. Not much better was the play that followed, *The Murder Game* by Board member Constance Cox.

Again the theatre closed throughout June and, Liz Pearson having moved on, a new General Manager arrived, Russell Hills, who had been running the Theatre Royal at Lincoln.

1976 was the famous 'long hot summer' which affected attendances at all theatres. The only show to do any good during that summer was *Tarantara-Tarantara,* the story of Gilbert and Sullivan, which featured Stratford Johns and Thomas Round.

Andrew Sachs, who began his career as assistant stage manager with the Overture Players, returned to the Connaught in 1977 to star in his own play, The Stamp Collector.
With him in the cast were Avril Angers and Su Pollard

The biggest success of the year was the arrival of John Howe as catering manager. A jazz enthusiast, he organised a series of concerts in the bar on nights when the theatre was 'dark'. Financed by outside sponsors, *Jazz on a Dark Night* attracted musicians of the calibre of Humphrey Lyttleton and Danny Moss. Large audiences enjoyed these evenings which produced a useful income.

In November the Borough Council agreed to increase its grant for 1977 to £30,000 and, since it looked as though there would be a deficit in the current year of around £8,000 (of which the Arts Council would cover £3,000), it agreed to pick up the tab for the balance.

The increased grant boosted confidence and in February 1977 it was announced that there would be no June closure - but if there was to be a break it would come after the pantomime. An exciting programme right through to Christmas was announced: as it turned out, only five of the eleven productions materialized - the other six were replaced by a succession of new plays, mainly with star names. The result was disastrous.

Derek Nimmo returned, this time with Sylvia Syms, in *Who Gets the Curtains?* This was another co-production with Ray Cooney (whose connection with the Connaught went back to 1949 when as a 16-year-old actor, he had appeared with the Overture Players in an American comedy, *Life with Father*). Although *Who Gets the Curtains?* did not work well in this production, Cooney had a great success with it when he re-shaped it and re-titled it *Wife Begins at Forty.*

It was followed by Max Frisch's *The Fire Raisers* which played, on average, to 74 people per performance. Then came Peggy Mount and Hugh Lloyd in a dire farce,

Porter Must Go, for which it was not unusual to hand out over 150 complementary tickets each night. Richard Todd appeared in a better drama, *The Heat of the Moment,* which collected respectable audiences, but *The Stamp Collector*, written by and starring Andrew Sachs with Avril Angers and Su Pollard, sent ticket sales to the bottom of the graph.

The most successful premieres were both musicals. The first British stage production of the musical version of *Gigi* featured Natalie Caron (cousin of Leslie Caron who had played the role in the film) and filled the theatre several times. In October Paul Jones appeared in *Drake's Dream,* a show primarily aimed at children, which transferred to London for the Christmas season.

That autumn the Connaught's funds were boosted by a lottery run by the Theatre Club and by £400 which was raised from various events organised by a local pub.

Joseph and the Technicolor Dreamcoat, staged in January, 1978, was seen by over 10,000 which helped the average attendance per performance over the financial year to creep up to 253, an increase of 60 over the previous year.

In order to reduce expenditure it was decided that from the end of March until the middle of June touring productions would be brought into the theatre. This was a policy which Russell Hills had successfully followed during his time in Lincoln.

The season opened with the *Rosemary Squire Show* but apart from a respectable production of Michael Frayn's recent success *Donkey's Years,* with Liz Fraser, and the appearance of *Coronation Street*'s Pat Phoenix in *My Cousin Rachel*, the shows did not appeal. By and large standards were poor, with several second-rate, cheap productions and some strange selections. Did anyone really believe the Belt and Braces Roadshow Company's three-hour polemic, *A Day in the Life of the World,* would find an audience in Worthing? Despite some extra funding from Southern Arts Association for one or two of the shows it was another financial disaster.

Such a disaster that by October it was obvious so much had been lost on the tours a deficit of at least £11,000 by the following March was inevitable. An approach was made to the Arts Council for something over and above the £50,000 grant for the year. The response was that Worthing Council should do more - as a result of inflation the local authority's subsidy had dropped from 25% of income to only 13%. Faced with these statistics the Borough agreed to put its grant up to £40,000.

In-house productions had come back in July with Alan Ayckbourn's trilogy, *The Norman Conquests,* which subsequently made a short tour. There was a lavish revival of *My Fair Lady*. Arthur Askey and his daughter, Anthea, recreated the roles they had originally played twenty-five years earlier in *The Love Match*. Unfortunately, during the run Arthur Askey suffered a severe heart attack and several performances had to be abandoned before a replacement could be found.

A revival of *Joseph* was as successful as on its original showing only ten months earlier and it cut its costs by going on to Bromley for a fortnight. Then came something not seen for a long time: a bout of public protest. The cause this time was the essential nude scene in Peter Shaffer's fine play, *Equus*. There were the now inevitable letters to the press and one councillor called for the ending of the Connaught's grant even though he had not seen the play to find out whether it was offensive.

Inflation caused another problem in July when Russell Hills left Worthing for the Empire Theatre in Sunderland where he was to be paid almost twice as much as the Connaught was offering. The Board advertised the post of General Manager, still at

£4,000 a year, but it was November before Makki Marseilles was tempted from the Palace, Watford, at the increased figure of £5,000 plus £750 in expenses.

Meanwhile the council had decided to reinstate the structure of the Pier Pavilion, work which would take three years from Easter, 1979. Most events were to be transferred to the Assembly Hall but some of the amateur groups preferred the idea of using the Connaught until they learned the hire charges - £2,000 a week in the autumn or £900 in spring. Despite protests, some did move to the Connaught, others used the makeshift facilities of the Assembly Hall.

In addition to his entertainments in the bar, John Howe conceived a new idea, holiday tours. Three-night holidays, inclusive of hotel, theatre ticket and travel to and from Worthing were to be marketed throughout the United Kingdom and in some continental areas such as Northern France and Belgium. The plan, launched in August, did not take off like *Jazz on a Dark Night:* the first travellers were three ladies who came from Romford at the end of the following April - there were no more.

By January, 1979, it was apparent that the theatre was in a critical financial position. Indications were that the deficit by the end of March could be as high as £15,000 plus £6,000 brought forward from the previous balance sheet. In a report to the Borough Council the Connaught's Board said that to prevent the theatre stumbling from crisis to crisis it needed £41,000 more than the current total subsidy of £90,000. Another approach was made to the Arts Council for more; again it was turned down though it was promised that the 1979/1980 grant would be increased in line with inflation to £57,000. After further negotiation, the Borough Council agreed to set aside £10,000 to create a contingency fund.

As soon as the pantomime season ended audiences plummeted. 1979 looked like being a bad year - it was.

Amateurs occupied the theatre for three shows in the spring and in June the first of a series of drastic decisions was made: plans to stage *The Merchant of Venice* in the autumn were scrapped. West Sussex County Council was told that unless it increased its contribution to the Theatre-in-Education tours they would cease and, finally, the Theatre Club was told to raise £1,000 for the theatre.

The summer was devoted to three plays, *Bedful of Foreigners, Bedroom Farce* and *The Bed Before Yesterday* which, under the composite title 'Bedtime at the Connaught', played in repertoire. Once again Worthing showed its dislike of the repertoire system and audiences were sparse. By July the situation was becoming

Arthur Askey and his daughter, Anthea, launched the ill-fated Connaught Theatre Holidays in August 1978

grave, it seemed unlikely that the theatre could survive. A local entrepreneur, Myles Byrne, thought he could devise a rescue plan and held talks with the Board but he soon pulled out.

By September it was obvious that between £12,000 and £14,000 was needed to stay open until Christmas. Yet another approach was made to the Arts Council with the usual result. It seemed certain that the theatre must close on 17 November, after the run of *Dr. Faustus,* a production sponsored by the Southern Television Trust. The Christmas show, *Peter Pan*, for which Sally Thomsett had been contracted, would have to be cancelled.

The Theatre Club organised the inevitable petition to keep the theatre open and got 14,000 signatures. Eventually rescue came when the Borough Council agreed to hand over the entire £10,000 in the contingency fund and to increase its subsidy to £50,000. Although *Peter Pan* was saved the Connaught would definitely close in January, possibly permanently.

A series of Sunday evening concerts had been arranged for the summer which caused unfortunate publicity when Richard Rodney Bennett, who was to accompany Marian Montgomery, refused to play the piano because it was not up to standard and the evening, which had sold well, was cancelled at the last moment.

Now another Sunday show caused trouble. A concert to boost funds was organised for 2 December. Peggy Mount, Hugh Lloyd and the cast of *Oh Calcutta!* (nude?) had agreed to appear. But the Board Chairman, Cllr Mrs Winifred Frampton, cancelled it fearing a flop since it transpired that the Society of West End Theatre Awards were being presented that night (not to mention that the Royal Variety Show was being shown on television at the same time!). According to local theatre enthusiast, Roy Wilson, he had phoned Jessie Matthews in Los Angeles and persuaded her to fly over for the show: when she heard of the cancellation she was alleged to have remarked, 'if they muck artists about like that they deserve to close.'

(This came to her ears when she returned from America and she immediately wrote to the Connaught's General Manager, Makki Marseilles, that not only had she not been contacted but she was booked to appear in Santa Monica on 2 December. Having appeared as a guest for Gillam, she was anxious to help keep the Connaught open and offered to give her services for a show at some mutually convenient date; but, sadly, she died before arrangements could be made.)

Peter Pan went ahead as planned, playing to record houses of 96%.

The theatre closed on 26 January 1980.

CHAPTER ELEVEN

Whilst the Connaught was closed, with the possibility of future government cuts in funding, the Drama Director of the Arts Council was looking at areas where savings could be made. His conclusion was that some regional companies would find their grants axed - and Worthing was one. If, however, the Connaught did reopen in the coming financial year its grant for 1981/82 was safe.

At the same time there were suggestions to the Board that possibly the Connaught should give up producing its own shows and become a Civic Theatre, used by amateurs and for buying-in touring productions. The suggestion was vigorously opposed.

The Board decided to recommence productions from 11 June 1980, running for at least 37 weeks. Since Makki Marseilles' contract as General Manager was due to expire in March the post was to be advertised and a Marketing Manager was also to be appointed to 'sell' the theatre as dynamically as possible.

As it turned out, the theatre did reopen before 11 June, several times. First, on 3 March, a touring production of Agatha Christie's *The Unexpected Guest* came in, with two favourites from Gillam's time, Peter Byrne and Richard Coleman. There was another touring show and a couple of amateur productions.

Among those who applied for the General Manager's job was a local man, David Turner. Careerwise, Turner was the antithesis of Bill Fraser; born into a theatrical family - his father was the stage manager of the Savoy Theatre, Kettering - he had trained for the stage but opted for a commercial career.

Passionately interested in theatre, soon after he arrived in the town he founded the Worthing Light Opera Company for whom, twice a year, he directed a large-scale musical. His success with these soon became talked about in NODA, the leading association of amateur musical theatre societies. Before long he was invited to direct shows for societies further afield and for this he was paid a fee and his expenses. As the demand for his services grew he felt secure enough to turn what had been a hobby into a full-time occupation, and he left the world of commerce to direct popular successes such as *Showboat, Oklahoma* and Gilbert and Sullivan favourites for amateur companies in places as farflung as Dublin and York.

Worthing remained his base: he went to the Connaught regularly and as often as possible he would go over to Brighton to catch the shows at the Theatre Royal. Here he met Melville Gillam.

The thought of running a theatre had never crossed his mind until one evening when Gillam phoned him at home:

'The Connaught wants a General Manager,' said Gillam.

'I know,' replied Turner.

'Well, have you got your application in?'

'I couldn't run the Connaught,' protested the amazed Turner, 'I haven't got the experience.'

'Oh, yes you could,' countered Gillam, 'You're the only person I know who could do the job. You know Worthing, you know what Worthing audiences want - go out and give it to them!'

Turner thought about it, decided he had nothing to lose and applied for the post. Any little hope he had of running the theatre vanished when he learned that he was

Michael Denison and Dulcie Gray in The Kingfisher *(1981). The set was one of the last designed by Ken Turner. Turner was a local boy who began his career at the Connaught in the 1950s and went on to design for most of the major repertory companies as well as working on a number of London productions*

to be the first of the ten applicants to be interviewed. The Board and their advisers formed an interview panel of sixteen, frightening enough for an experienced man of the theatre, unnerving for someone on the fringe of the business.

That both he and the success of the Worthing Light Opera Company were known to the chairman, Winnie Frampton, and most of the Board undoubtedly acted in his favour and to his surprise he was appointed.

Nic Young, too, was delighted. He knew Turner and on several occasions in the bar they had amicably discussed the Connaught's problems.

Turner became General Manager on 1 May, 1980.

The appointment of a Marketing Manager was delayed until the new General Manager had had a chance to see the list of applicants and help in drawing up a short list. The eventual choice was Ann-Marie Spolton who arrived on 8 June and left two months later, staying slightly longer than the new front of house manager, Peter Heriot, who went after six weeks.

The first night of the reopening production, *An Ideal Husband,* was a glittering affair. Starring Philip Bond, Eunice Grayson and Christopher Scoular, it played to 8,200 and showed a profit of £1,000 in its three-and-a-half-week run. A few weeks later Eunice Grayson returned to appear in a lavish production of the musical, *Kismet*, which was seen by 11,510.

Aimi Macdonald played the title role in *The Prime of Miss Jean Brodie* which pulled in almost 7,500 patrons. Audiences had more than doubled over the same period last year and it looked as though the new organisation was a success. An innovation of Turner's was to launch a subscription scheme for tickets. There were over 2,000 subscribers for the first season of four productions bringing in an advance income of just under £10,000.

In the absence of a Marketing Manager a Publicity Officer was deemed desirable. There were sixty applications for the post which went to Terry Rickwood, another member of the Worthing Light Opera Company and a close friend of Turner.

Tom Stoppard's *Jumpers* was staged in October with Macdonald Hobley and an actor from the early days of the Chris Denys regime, Ellis Jones, who stayed on to direct a nine-week tour by the Theatre-in-Education team.

At the end of four months the Connaught was doing so well that the Borough Council made a point of congratulating the Governors on their success.

In October a visit by London City Ballet sold 3,669 of the 4,240 seats available. This was followed by the appearances of Nyree Dawn Porter and Christopher Neame in *The Taming of the Shrew;* then came *Godspell* and for Christmas Christopher Biggins in *Toad of Toad Hall.* There was sponsorship of £2,500 for this production from the Gateway Building Society.

There was no need to contemplate closure that winter and guest stars with the resident players included Bill Simpson, Michael Denison, Dulcie Gray and Robert Flemyng. During the 39-week season audiences totalled 113,306 (73% capacity) and there was a surplus for the year of over £20,000.

It was with understandable pride that the Connaught announced that it had been promoted from a Grade 3 to a Grade 2 theatre by the Theatre Managers' Association

Buster Merryfield was straight out of drama school when he began his professional acting career at the Connaught. He is seen here in Nic Young's 1979 production of Michael Frayn's comedy Alphabetical Order. *With him are Alec Wallis, Tricia Thorns and Pamela Pitchford*

and Equity, the actors' union. It was not, however, mentioned that the actors' wages would have to go up as a result. The one sad note was the death, on Christmas Day, of Melville Gillam at his home in Brighton.

The annual pantomimes had made money but they were not of a very high standard. Invariably played by the resident company with the addition of one or two artistes from the world of light entertainment, the problem was usually the script. People are happy to have a crack at writing a panto script without realising what a specialised art it is. Certainly the standard of the Christmas shows rose from 1979 when *Peter Pan* was staged. This was followed by *Toad of Toad Hall* and *The Wizard of Oz*. David Turner then staged two better pantomimes in *Cinderella* and *Dick Whittington*, before producing, in succession, two remarkably appropriate Christmas shows, *Annie* and *Oliver!*.

And so, through 1981, success followed success. Jean Anderson and Dora Bryan featured among the guest players, and the subscription scheme was a resounding success with over 3,300 tickets being taken up for a season which included such varied works as *Arsenic and Old Lace*, Vanburgh's *The Provok'd Wife*, *The Dame of Sark, The Dresser* and the musical, *Gypsy*. Everything was, in the words of one of the numbers from that show, coming up roses. Until October.

Although the theatre had been enjoying great success, inflation was causing problems again. Expenditure had risen by 64.5% but income (box office, Arts Council and local authority) had gone up by only 59.4%.

Once again the Board had to go cap in hand to the Borough Council: unless between £10,000 and £15,000 more was made available the theatre would have to close for another three months after Christmas. It was the upgrading which was to blame - the Board now realised that this 'honour' was costing so much in actors' wages that seat prices should have been raised as soon as it was bestowed.

Reluctantly the council agreed to give up to £10,800 as a guarantee against loss in addition to the basic subsidy of £56,500, but it insisted that the theatre must put its house in order. It also called for a report on the likely situation for 1982/83.

The Board presented its report in January. It needed an increase in its grant to £100,000. The council was tightening its belt and replied that it was unlikely to be able to find more than £68,000. So costs had to be cut and hard decisions had to be made. First, the annual Shakespearean production would have to go, to be replaced by something cheaper. Second, unless there was a huge increase in audiences, the theatre would close for nine and a half weeks after the pantomime. The main economy, however, was to abolish the posts of Artistic Director and his part-time secretary.

There was considerable concern among many of the Trustees at the dismissal of the Artistic Director without reference to them. Some questioned whether the Arts Council was likely to continue to subsidise a regional theatre without an Artistic Director. Yes, said the Chairman of the Board. Unlikely, said Stephen Boyce, the Southern Arts Association representative.

In fact, the Arts Council wrote to the Board expressing considerable concern at the move and, whilst it did not have any definite rules for the running of a theatre, it felt artistic continuity was as important as administrative continuity. 'It is important,' wrote the Drama Director, 'that the Council should fully understand what it is being asked to subsidise.' This was the beginning of a long and rarely

Some of the orphans in the 1984 production of Annie

satisfactory correspondence which ended only with the publication of the Arts Council's 'Glory of the Garden' strategy.

Councillors, too, were not happy at developments and costs at the Connaught, some pressing for an independent inquiry. At a full council meeting this was turned down in favour of a further report from the Board.

When the financial results for the year 1980/81 were revealed, it was found that the previous year's surplus had been negated by a deficit of £21,012.

Nic Young's final production, *Cider with Rosie,* opened on 21 April 1982. Unlike his predecessors, he did not leave the area but set up the Rainbow Theatre Company to continue his work among children.

At Easter the Pier Pavilion reopened after its highly expensive facelift, just as the council announced that in the last year the Assembly Hall had cost £1/4 million to run.

On stage at the Connaught visitors continued to appear. Jean Kent and Patrick Barr appeared in *Dear Octopus*, then came Terence Longden, Dilys Watling, Hildegard Neil, Richard Coleman, Dora Bryan and Dermot Walsh. Pip Hinton came back for *No, No Nanette.* The plays chosen were run-of-the-mill, with no risks being taken, and though the pantomime, *Cinderella* with Bobby Crush, achieved 84% capacity, the overall figure until the theatre's closure on 22 January 1983 was 56.3% - unfortunately at least 63% was needed to break even.

There was no doubt that musicals were popular and brought in large audiences, but they were very expensive to stage. Even the 71% capacity which *No, No Nanette* played to was insufficient to cover its costs. In an endeavour to maximise income from these productions, David Turner was constantly pressurising commercial managements to take them over and tour them to some of the large provincial theatres. Great interest was shown but a major problem was that the idiosyncrasies of the Connaught's stage made it necessary for sets to be rebuilt and enlarged, making a tour uneconomic. On the odd occasion when a 'number one' tour was seriously contemplated negotiations were usually nearing completion stage when someone - usually the American copyright-holders - put up an insoluble problem.

The cast of the 1982 revival of Dodie Smith's Dear Octopus *was headed by Patrick Barr and Jean Kent*

Had any of these tours materialized the Connaught might have avoided the financial problems which confronted it.

The limelight this year, however, was rarely focused on the stage but on finances, politics and even food. In October the Board decided to ban amateurs from hiring the theatre despite the charges having risen to £2,500 a week plus 5% of the gross takings and wages to some staff members. David Turner said the ban was because of plans to launch a new super show at Worthing after the reopening. (He was, at that stage, negotiating with Nottingham Playhouse for a co-production of the British premiere of Stephen Sondheim's *Follies*. After playing seasons at Worthing and Nottingham it was planned to take it into the West End. Negotiations with Sondheim's New York office were protracted and the costs rose week by week. Eventually it became obvious that the cost would be too high for the Connaught which pulled out. The entire project was eventually aborted.) At the same time, there was truth in many people's belief that the embargo's real purpose was to force the amateurs back to the pier and after considerable protests from the societies the ban was lifted.

Meanwhile the Egon Ronay *Good Food Guide* inspectors had been doing the rounds of theatre catering. The Connaught was slammed as providing inferior convenience food in a dreary restaurant. It was termed a 'charade', though there was praise for the friendly staff. (The Connaught was not the only theatre attacked for its catering - another 21 were in the same boat!)

During the closure, plans were being made for the financial year 1983/84 when it was realised that going dark for fifteen weeks was not going to solve the problem for the current year. The budgeted box office income had been £237,000 but less than £218,000 had been achieved. The Borough Council was approached again and a new deal was hammered out. The debt was cleared, the council would match the

Arts Council grant of £74,000 and a further £10,000 would be put into reserve against a possible deficit.

Plans for the coming year were devised. First, Bob Gunnell, recently retired from BBC local radio, was appointed part-time Marketing Manager and Turner persuaded Anna Neagle to play in the opening production, Coward's *Relative Values.*

Whilst closed the theatre had been rewired, the stage floor replaced and the dressing rooms redecorated. Bob Gunnell set about attracting sponsorship with the launch of a brochure, 'Working with the Connaught', which did have some success.

The opening night of *Relative Values,* on 11 May 1983, was a gala occasion: a piano tinkled in the foyer and dinner jackets were requested (this aroused resentment from several theatregoers who considered it a relic of the past).

Turner was making an impression in the theatre world: after Anna Neagle came Muriel Pavlow, Michael Denison and Dulcie Gray again, Avril Angers, Eleanor Summerfield and Paul Maxwell. In the height of the summer Edmund Hockridge and Hilary Tindall appeared in *South Pacific* (seen by 13,000). Other productions that season included *A Doll's House*, *Educating Rita* and, importantly, the British premiere of *On Golden Pond* which Turner had negotiated while on a brief holiday in New York.

The stars were back, not only on stage but, as in Gillam's time, well-known faces were to be seen in the stalls. Among those who saw Connaught productions were Derek Jacobi, Brenda Bruce, Marti Webb, Dame Flora Robson, Susan George, Ian Ogilvy and Elizabeth Allen.

Edmund Hockridge and Isla St Clair with the children in The Sound of Music *(1984)*

More importantly the top managements which Turner had been courting were coming to Worthing again. Duncan Weldon, Bill Kenwright, Mark Furness and Sir Peter Saunders saw a number of productions.

The bar was causing problems. Since the publication of the Egon Ronay report takings had begun to drop and by November it was losing £100 a week. It was decided to hand the operation over to outside caterers.

There were some changes on the Board of Governors when

Cllr Stanley Elliott became chairman and recently elected member Sidney Burton, former Managing Director of the Gateway Building Society, his deputy.

In the autumn the Board told the Borough Council that the theatre was on course to achieve its budget for nine months and with an extra £21,000 it could stay open after the pantomime. This request was definitely a 'one off' which would not be repeated. Not a grant, but a guarantee for that amount was approved.

When the financial year ended there was a deficit of £11,431, almost £10,000 less than anticipated. The audience capacity for the year had averaged 55%.

There was another 'honour', less costly this time, when the Connaught won the 1983 Worthing Publicity Award for bringing the 'big names' to the town.

The financial year 1984/85 started disastrously.

The Arts Council had completed its review of funding strategy and, as had been foreshadowed, decided to make some significant changes which would affect its regional theatre clients. Some were to continue to receive public funding, not from the Arts Council, but via their Regional Arts Associations, others were to receive nothing. The Connaught was to get nothing. Worthing was to be weeded out of the Arts Council's 'garden' on 1 April 1985.

The Board was determined to keep the theatre open. First they called for help from the local MP, Terence Higgins, who undertook to meet the chairman of the Arts Council. They also decided to send a deputation to London and to organise a petition.

The Arts Council's response, on 18 May, was typically arrogant and demanded that further evidence of the need for a grant be despatched within fourteen days or a deputation would be pointless.

The necessary statistics were supplied without delay and, on 17 July, Sidney Burton with three colleagues from the Board had an hour's meeting with the Secretary General of the Arts Council, Luke Ritner. During the discussions they handed over a petition of nearly 7,000 signatures. Their appeal, they were told, would be considered by the full council at its next meeting.

Alas, the appeal was turned down, the Connaught being one of only two theatres not to have their grants reinstated. The reason given was that the local authority was not contributing enough, but did the absence of an Artistic Director and the lack of an annual Shakespearean production have any bearing on the withdrawal of funding? Very probably.

Stanley Elliott was not only chairman of the Connaught's Board but also of the Borough Council's powerful Policy and Resources Committee. He was adamant that the theatre must continue to function and was quoted in the press, 'A live theatre is so important and any successful town should have one.'

By August the Board had decided its policy: there were to be joint productions with other regional theatres, West End previews and sponsorship from local companies. Even so, they acknowledged that the theatre would have to go dark for three months of the year.

The plans were put to the Policy and Resources Committee at their September meeting where the vote was 8 to 6 in favour of an increase in the subsidy for 1985/86 of £57,000, bringing it to £131,000. This was backed at the subsequent full Council meeting by 21-10 votes. This, it was hoped, would be sufficient for the Connaught to stay open for 42 weeks. (Compared to the town's other amenities the investment was modest: the Assembly Hall was costing £198,000

Lockwood West (Timothy West's father) in William Douglas Home's last play, And As for Jonathan, *directed by David Turner in a set by John Hilder (1985)*

that year, the Pier Pavilion £358,000 and the Aquarena swimming complex £462,000.)

A reception for local businesses was held at the Town Hall, hosted by Lavinia, Duchess of Norfolk, to promote sponsorship. Although it was not to get an Arts Council grant, the theatre would be eligible for an award under the new Business Sponsorship Incentive scheme whereby, when businesses were persuaded to sponsorship for the first time, an additional amount would come from State funds.

Meanwhile the Board had agreed to appoint David Turner as the Theatre Director for a two-year experimental period during which he would be responsible for directing one third of the productions.

The first of his productions was *The Sound of Music* which ran throughout August starring Edmund Hockridge again, this time with Isla St Clair. It was seen by 19,000 people who paid more than £95,000 at the box office, producing a profit in excess of £5,000.

In October, however, most of that was wiped out with a co-production of *Lady Windermere's Fan* which had come from the Theatre Royal, Windsor. During a run of three and a half weeks it played to only 41% capacity.

The Christmas show, *Annie*, did even better than *The Sound of Music*, putting over 20,000 bums on the seats. By the end of the financial year the deficit was only £142 (Value Added Tax payments during the year had amounted to £47,832!)

After the run of *The Sound of Music*, the Connaught was let to a local company, Downland Opera, for four performances of *The Marriage of Figaro*. Although the production left much to be desired, the principal roles were sung by students of the Royal College of Music. As soon as the overture ended and Figaro and Susannah opened the opera it was obvious to many that they were listening to a baritone voice of astounding quality: since his Connaught debut Gerald Finley has repeated the role at Glyndebourne, Covent Garden and Los Angeles.

That autumn it was deemed desirable to appoint an Administrator to run the theatre and allow David Turner to concentrate on the directing side. Bob Gunnell resigned from his part-time marketing work and early in 1985 Rodney Cake was appointed Administrator, handling publicity, marketing and promotion.

Turner was not at the interview when Cake was selected for the post. Within days of his arrival the Connaught was in uproar and discontent was rife. Soon every one of the employees had given in their notice. The Board could not allow the situation to continue and Cake resigned.

There had been a constant turnover of staff, often as a result of personality clashes, but this departure was acrimonious and public. The local press reported Cake as saying he had received no cooperation from Turner, who had 'no intention of parting with any of his duties or relinquishing any of his power.'

The fact that the Board had paid £2,000 compensation to terminate Cake's contract was not, however, made public. Letters and comments to the press showed that the public was concerned at the situation despite assurances from Lewis Elliott, secretary to the Theatre's Trust (and, of course, Chief Executive of the Borough Council), that 'Mr. Turner is doing a good job of work at the Connaught in difficult circumstances and has the full support of the Board of Governors in doing so.'

But it had created an unpleasant atmosphere in the town and the box office suffered badly.

During the early part of the first year without Arts Council funding audiences fluctuated. In his report to the Trustees, Stanley Elliott warned that the loss of the grant was serious and that 'It is not possible to say that the theatre's continued existence is, as yet, secure.'

One of the first productions was *And As for Jonathan* by William Douglas Home which had been premiered a few months earlier at Farnham. The author was not happy with it, realising it needed a lot of rewriting. Having seen productions of his *Kingfisher* and *The Dame of Sark* at Worthing he was impressed by developments and he asked Turner to go to Farnham and put forward suggestions for improvements in his latest work. Despite its homosexual theme, it played to a moderate 4,500 at

Patrick Mower starred in Ivor Novello's Perchance to Dream, *the spectacular fiftieth anniversary production which opened on 30 September 1985*

More young orphans, this time in Oliver! *the last regular 'in house' production staged at the Connaught (December 1985)*

Worthing which was very much better than audiences for *The Deep Blue Sea* and *Romantic Comedy* which saw figures drop to 3,512 and 3,471 respectively.

Nevertheless there was an air of optimism around for this was the Connaught's fiftieth anniversary year and plans had been made for a big celebration with a month's run of Ivor Novello's *Perchance to Dream,* starring Patrick Mower. Following the success of *Annie, Oliver!* was scheduled for Christmas.

Although not quite up to target before the opening of the summer musical, *The King and I,* success seemed assured and it seemed there was a reasonable hope that the theatre would be able to stay open all the year round. But although 15,000 people saw Lorna Dallas and Mark Wynter in *The King and I,* this was too few to cover the costs of the production. Suddenly the shortfall for the year had jumped to £33,000.

After the musical came Noel Coward's *South Sea Bubble* with Barbara Murray, Glyn Houston and Pauline Jameson. The build-up to the Jubilee celebrations had begun.

Planning for the great occasion had started over twelve months earlier. The local department store, Bentalls, was sponsoring *Perchance to Dream* and also hosting the gala first night festivities.

The show itself was to be followed by a short scene from *Dear Octopus* played by a distinguished cast which included Dorothy Primrose, Anna Neagle, Dora Bryan, Margaretta Scott and Lockwood West. William Douglas Home, who had worked at the theatre for a while with Bill Fraser, had written an 'oration'. After all this everyone would move across to the Assembly Hall for a champagne reception and ball.

The big night was Monday, 30 September, fifty years to the day since Bill Fraser moved his company into the New Connaught Theatre and, in company with Daniel

Massey and Dorothy Primrose, he attended a thanksgiving service at St. Paul's church the previous afternoon.

The night itself was a glittering success, even though not every seat was sold. At the Assembly Hall the champagne flowed and they danced the night away. The hangover, when it began, was painful and serious.

Perchance to Dream was a disappointing production and there had been backstage disagreements which had not helped. Over the four weeks it played to 10,238 people (60%), insufficient to cover costs. By the end of the run the accumulated shortfall was heading towards £40,000.

It was quite obvious now that the theatre would have to close after the Christmas show, but in the meantime provision had to be made for the debts. The Board went to the council. The Policy and Resources Committee voted 7-6 to clear any outstanding balance but it refused a request for an additional £16,000 to enable the theatre to stay open between January and March. The sting was in the tail: it voted to make no grant whatever for the following year, a decision which Stanley Elliott would try to overturn at the next full council meeting.

Just weeks before the meeting three new Borough Councillors had been appointed governors to replace those retiring from the Board. They were not happy with David Turner's style, nor with his personnel management. They saw him still as an 'amateur' and did not want him to continue running the theatre. An unholy alliance was formed with their council colleagues who could see no reason why the Connaught should exist anyway.

On 7 November 1985, a heated debate lasted for over two hours and by 23 votes to 8 the council decided to discontinue the grant to the Worthing and District Connaught Theatre Ltd. The news was passed to a crowd of more than 200 supporters outside the council chamber. They were dismayed: the Connaught was dead.

In fact it was not - quite. A working party was to be formed to look at ways of maintaining live theatre in the town and was to report back in February, before the

The Connaught after its 1986 'facelift'

1986/87 budget was decided. The dissenting Connaught Governors were appointed to serve on the working party; their chairman, Stanley Elliott, was not.

The theatrical profession was horrified at the council's decision. Anna Neagle had intended to be at the council meeting but illness prevented it. The matter was raised at meetings of the Theatre Managers Association and Equity who were both powerless.

Throughout the final weeks well-known actors brought condolences to the staff. Michael Denison referred to Turner as an outstanding theatre director, adding 'This is a classic example of a theatre becoming a political pawn. Unfortunately, in all but a very few cases the good men and true of local councils are not the best suited to run theatres. They require a theatrical element to help.'

The final night, on 18 January, 1986, bore little resemblance to the final nights of either Fraser or Gillam. Then there were no curtain speeches, no farewells; this time the capacity audience and the thirty staff about to lose their jobs heard a long and passionate speech from David Turner.

For the staff it was particularly heart-breaking; many people had found they could not work with Turner and left quickly, but the hard core supported him throughout. They did not grumble at working long hours without overtime payment, for Turner was there with them working even longer hours. Their common bond was their love of the Connaught.

Like so many before him, Turner was to find that his time at the Connaught was not wasted, for it was here that he met Sir Peter Saunders, for whose company he became General Manager.

The second phase of the Connaught had lasted just over eighteen turbulent years. What next?

CHAPTER TWELVE

Inevitably, as soon as the closure was announced the protests, petitions and rescue campaigns began. The major event this time was bizarre.

Two brothers, Roy and Michael Wilson, announced their intention to go on hunger strike to save the theatre. They attracted world-wide publicity as much, it seemed, for themselves as for the theatre. Not everyone in the theatre world was behind them, following the Jessie Matthews debacle six years earlier. As their exploits received more and more attention the vast majority of Worthing ratepayers, who did not give a jot whether or not the theatre survived, became nauseated by the whole affair.

Although the Wilsons claimed the credit for saving the Connaught, they were, in reality, nothing more than an irrelevant nuisance. If the theatre was saved by anyone it was by Patrick Boyd Maunsell.

The brief for the 'Live Theatre Working Party' was to examine the future of theatre in Worthing. The three former Connaught Governors who had voted against the continuation of the grant were amongst the seven members of the working party and their leader, Cllr Tony MacMillan, was appointed chairman.

His perception of the theatre's future was detailed to the press a few days after the controversial vote: 'I took a lot of flak for my vote - some people accused me of killing the Connaught. But my vote was against the grant and for live theatre.

'I would like to see a Connaught that is alive all the time and not just for performances.

'It needs more of almost everything. If the Odeon cinema is going to close, the theatre should show films on a Sunday. It could be a venue for jazz concerts and art shows.

'It should have activities going on in the bar, even when a show is in progress. It needs far better marketing than it has at present. We should make more of an amenity that is very important to the town - we need live theatre.'

The first major decision made by the group was to call in an independent theatre consultant to investigate the position. If he agreed with their proposition that live theatre was essential to the town he would be able to persuade their less sanguine colleagues on the council more easily than they themselves could.

With council agreement to spend up to £5,000, on the recommendation of the Southern Arts Association, early in January Patrick Boyd Maunsell was asked to prepare a report as a matter of urgency. The former director of the Key Theatre, Peterborough, and administrator of the Theatre Royal, Bury St. Edmunds, within two weeks he met 42 groups and interested individuals to ascertain what they

Meanwhile half a dozen managements were showing interest in working with the Connaught, most notably Michael Croft, who was looking for a base for his National Youth Theatre.

Also keenly watching events was the Arts Minister, Richard Luce, whose parliamentary constituency, Shoreham-by-Sea, abutted Worthing. In view of the 'arm's length' principle, he was unable to exert any influence on the Arts Council to reconsider the withdrawal of the Connaught's grant. But he did make approaches to Southern Arts Association and was in constant contact with Worthing's own MP, Terence Higgins. Higgins, for his part, felt it was important that the Connaught should remain a producing theatre and not become a receiving house.

Boyd Maunsell's proposals were put to the Working Party early in February. The recommendations were that the theatre 'should have a strong drama base, but be wide-ranging; a clear identity is needed which will fully complement the promotion of the pier and the Assembly Hall.'

'The programme,' he continued, 'needs to be sufficiently predictable to build trust, but never so predictable as to be dull. The aim is to create a very large audience that comes to the theatre about four or five times a year.'

He proposed that the Connaught should be open for about 46 weeks a year, the 'dark' period to allow for maintenance, renewals and staff holidays.

The main feature was that there should be a resident company to provide eighteen weeks of productions per year, each running, usually, for two weeks, but longer for the Christmas and summer periods. The non-seasonal productions would tour to other venues. The resident company would be totally independent of the Borough Council's funding.

Ten weeks should be given over to taking major tours and twelve weeks to smaller-scale tours, opera, dance, children's shows and one-night stands Six weeks would be allocated to local amateurs at a subsidised rental.

The workshops should be made available to amateur societies, the bar would be open all day, there should be work for and with young people, films, conference facilities and a 'positive policy of generating ancillary income from full use of the building.'

'It should,' he concluded, 'be made easy and pleasant for the public to spend money in the Connaught.'

The proposals provided that the theatre should be run, not by a Trust as in the past, but as an independent company limited by guarantee and registered as a Charity. A council grant should cover the running of the theatre and its staffing, estimated at £200,000 a year. All other expenses would be met from operating income, which should be in excess of £350,000 a year.

Putting the proposals to the council, Tony MacMillan added that the twin keys to the future success of live theatre in Worthing were a professional management and a much greater community involvement.

The proposals were approved and a grant of £290,000 was agreed, considerably more than the Connaught had ever received from the local authority before. The Board of Directors was to consist of six sitting councillors, three non-council members nominated by the Borough and three other members nominated by the Board; the Secretary and Treasurer would be council officials. No rent or rates would be payable by the new company. It has to be said that when the Borough was called upon to nominate a non-council member to the Board it invariably sought advice from the rest of the directors. But the Board was too heavily politicised to be truly independent.

Work had to move apace to get the theatre reopened as soon as possible. The first decision was to restyle and renovate the building. Plans were already in hand for it to be rewired, now it was proposed to redesign the bar and turn it into a lively meeting place. The black and cream facade tiling, installed over fifty years before when the Picturedrome was converted into the Connaught, was crumbling and replacements were unobtainable. It was proposed that the exterior should be rendered and designed to merge into the architecture of nearby buildings. A slight alteration to the auditorium would increase accessibility but reduce seating capacity to 514.

The original Connaught Hall was to be converted from scenic, carpenters' and paint shops into a multi-purpose theatre workshop and a new, small bar was to be created in the foyer area.

The overall cost for these alterations was put at £235,000 and the aim was to have the work completed for a Christmas reopening.

The next step was to advertise the post of Administrator.

After all the excitement of leading the Working Party there was a nasty blow for Tony MacMillan when he lost his council seat at the local elections. As a result he had to leave the working party and his successor as chairman was Cllr Jonathan Chowen, who had been a Connaught Governor earlier in the 1980s.

On 1 September 1986, Martin Harris became the Connaught's Administrator. He had been variously company manager, production and technical manager and deputy administrator at Theatr Clwyd for more than ten years. He had also worked with Welsh National Opera and Dance Company in Cardiff, the Watermill Theatre at Newbury and the Victoria Theatre, Stoke-on-Trent. He certainly had a highly professional theatre background and it was announced that Patrick Boyd Maunsell would stay on for a few months to work with the new Administrator.

Speaking to the local press, Harris said the Connaught's problems were well-known within the theatre world, adding, with shades of Bell and Fraser, 'People even felt sorry for me when they knew I was coming here.'

There were echoes, too, of Chris Denys, when he said, 'Anyone thinking that the Connaught will be as they remember it will be disappointed. This is the time for change.'

By November the plans were finalised. Announcing that the theatre would reopen on 19 December 1986, with the pantomime *Mother Goose,* Jonathan Chowen spoke of the new Board of Directors who would be appointed.

'An air of professionalism has to be stamped on the Connaught. The game the Connaught is now in is too dangerous to be left to well-meaning amateurs.

'We are concerned about raising the standard and status of the Connaught and one of the ways to do this is to increase the standard of the management committee.'

Fittingly, Tony MacMillan was elected to the Board. From the world of theatre came Christopher Dunham, administrator of the New Theatre Portsmouth, Patrick Boyd Maunsell, Vanessa Ford, managing director of Vanessa Ford Productions, Sylvia Vickers (former director and South East Arts drama panellist), Millie Gorton, secretary of the Worthing and District Music Festival and well-known amongst the town's amateur societies, plus six Worthing councillors. Council officials remained as Company Secretary and Treasurer.

On 27 September 1986, the Odeon closed for redevelopment and the only cinema now left in Worthing was the old Picturedrome's adversary, the Dome, long past any prime it might once have enjoyed. The chances were that it, too, would soon be demolished for redevelopment.

A month later the council agreed to spend £31,000 on the latest cinema equipment for the Connaught, where it was expected films would fill 20% of the annual programme. One councillor thought it crazy to waste money in this way when it was obvious that cinemas everywhere were closing down through lack of interest.

Meanwhile Martin Harris was spending the autumn planning the programme to follow the pantomime, due to end a five-week season on 24 January. The first thing that was obvious to him was that there was no possibility whatever of starting a resident company for at least twelve months: the first year would have to consist entirely of bought-in products. He had plans, however, for providing a team of baby-sitters for parents who wanted an evening at the theatre and for staging contemporary dance in the former Connaught Hall, now to be known as 'the Ritz'.

By the middle of December Harris was able to announce plans for the winter season. There was to be free jazz in the bar on Saturday lunchtimes, a week of dance, both live and on film, and the drama season was due to open with *The Normal Heart,* a play about AIDS. For once there was no storm of outrage about such a subject, just a few mumblings of discontent.

Prior to the first night of the pantomime there was an official reopening of the Connaught to which 400 guests were invited. The mayor, Cllr Michael Parkin, was to have fired a laser gun to blast off a giant padlock and chain, but this was cancelled; however, fireworks lit the sky and the Worthing Silver Band played a specially composed march, entitled *'Connaught'.*

Inside, the guests admired the newly decorated and recarpeted auditorium, the upgraded dressing rooms and the new toilets, including one for the disabled. They trooped through the control room with its computerised lighting-board and then into the Ritz workshop which, although cleaned, had not been redecorated. Off then to the refurbished bar where Ken Lyon and his trio were playing amongst the potted palms. Here they noticed the biggest changes: a new servery had been built and the decor completely changed. Everything, they agreed, was splendid.

Cllr Chowen welcomed the guests, telling them that the Connaught was no longer just a theatre but a micro-arts centre willing to stage the very best of all arts with professional theatre as the cornerstone.

Mother Goose, directed by Dougie Squires, was one of the best pantomimes seen in Worthing for many, many years. Glittering, colourful and traditional, it had a dame par-excellence in Denny Willis and the well-known actor William Squire played the villain.

During its five-week run it enjoyed an audience of over 19,000 and made a profit of more than £20,000. No wonder that on the last night it was announced from the stage that the same management, Trends Organisation and the Jamie Phillips Group, would be returning the following Christmas to present *Aladdin*, again with Denny Willis.

Now the theatre could get down to real business - except that the tour of *The Normal Heart* had been abandoned and the Connaught went dark for a week.

Then came a week of *The Lion, the Witch and the Wardrobe,* presented by the Vanessa Ford management. The aim was to involve youngsters in the theatre and it certainly did - every seat was sold for the seven performances and another £1,500 added to the bank account.

Meanwhile Harris had set up youth theatre workshops, an 'outreach' department, a film society and organised a public open day. At all of these Harris himself was on show.

The first season was varied: there was Circus Senso, which combined rock music, acrobatics, puppetry, mime and dancing, the Jiving Lindyhoppers, Bob Kerr's Whoopee Band and an illustrated lecture on 'More Than 50 Years of Motor Racing'.

It was, however, drama that was to be the cornerstone of the Connaught. The directors, it seemed, had not realised it, neither Boyd Maunsell nor Harris could have known it, but ever since the Connaught had been in the chrysalis stage Worthing audiences had been firm in their distaste for touring plays. The disastrous season of 1932 had brought Bell and Fraser to the town, the lack of response to the wartime tours had driven Seebold to despair. Even Gillam could not get an audience to his pre-West End shows and in 1978 the touring season had almost brought about the closure of the theatre. Had audience attitudes changed?

The first drama, Cambridge Theatre Company's production of *Peer Gynt,* played to 1,265. *Charley's Aunt* the following week brought in 1,690 and *The Dresser* was seen by only 1,091. Between them the first three 'major' tours lost over £3,800.

Ballet Rambert had always done well in Worthing, so had recent visits by London City Ballet, how about the planned week of dance? Unfortunately the plans for a whole week fell apart and there was one performance by *La Bouche* (seen by 141 people) and the film *The Red Shoes*, which attracted 52. Nevertheless these shows cost little and the two produced about £200.

The first major film was *A Room with a View,* which played to 57% houses over nine showings and netted £1,900. The final booking of the financial year was Birmingham Music Theatre's production of *Madama Butterfly*, the first time that Worthing had seen wholly professional opera for many years. No matter what happened a loss was inevitable for this attraction. The cost, which included a 26-piece orchestra, was £7,950 for two nights: the maximum the Connaught could take was £4,917, but an occasional production of this nature was part of the new theatre's raison d'étre. The result was satisfactory, *Madama Butterfly* played to 90% capacity (924), and the loss of £3,700 was good value considering the prestige and the new audiences the production had brought in.

The Board of Directors and the council were understandably well pleased with the results of the first four months: the trading profit of over £13,000 was £7,000 more than budgeted and catering had added over £3,750.

The Worthing Herald, however, sounded a note of warning: 'The Council have put a colossal sum of money into the building. The public must continue to support it.

'A lesson from the past is that when the theatre reopened before under Chris Denys there were large audiences for *The Beggar's Opera* and subsequent productions. But they dwindled and slowly the theatre began its financial troubles.'

This time the troubles did not begin slowly.

In April 1987 eleven performances of the children's show, *Mr. Men's Magic Island* lost £2,400. The adult dramas *Month of Sundays* and *Corpse* each lost over £2,000 and Cambridge Theatre Company's production of Molière's *The Misanthrope*, which played to only 809, cost more than £4,000. Films made a small profit, but at the end of two months the trading loss was almost £12,500. By the end of July the figure had risen to £19,000. With help from the Borough Treasurer the loss, although not hidden, was not readily appreciated by the council or the press.

For the month of August a musical, *Sweet Charity,* was staged with Su Pollard and Jess Conrad in the leads. Though not as successful as previous summer musicals in terms of audience capacity, the show cost less and produced a handsome profit of £15,000. There were sighs of relief.

A series of films kept the takings on an even keel, but the first play of the autumn, *Twelfth Night,* was seen by 2,400 and lost £1,750. Three nights provided by Travelling Opera pulled in only 432 customers and lost over £3,000. By Christmas the loss was running at £3,450.

Aladdin rubbed his magic lamp to good effect and made almost £22,000. Suddenly, in the winter of 1988 it seemed that the theatre's fortunes were about to change: audiences increased, children's shows, films and three plays all did well and after the November loss of £19,000 the year ended with a profit of almost £29,000.

The next financial year started well, and by July there was a profit of almost £13,000. Again a summer musical was staged throughout August, *Guys and Dolls* with the ebullient Barbara Windsor and Christopher Biggins. This time, however, audiences were poor and the show lost nearly £8,000.

The most successful play that autumn was *To Kill a Mocking Bird* which played to 90% capacity and was seen by around 3,700 people. But with a large cast headed by Alan Dobie and Hildegard Neil it was expensive to stage, and the £13,624 that it took only just covered the costs.

Instead of pantomime, *Peter Pan* was staged at Christmas, making over £27,500, and a winter season of films like *A Fish Called Wanda* and plays such as *Night Must Fall* and *An Ideal Husband* sent the year's trading profits soaring to over £50,000.

In two and a quarter years trading the Connaught had made nearly £100,000. The council grant had now been cut to £220,000 but with good husbandry running costs had been lower than expected so an agreeable reserve could be tucked away. With a flourish of publicity the Directors returned £5,000 to the Borough Treasurer.

The bar was doing well, the Ritz

Both Barbara Windsor and Christopher Biggins were making return visits to the Connaught when they starred in the 1988 staging of Guys and Dolls

Beneath photographs of the theatre's founder, Bill Fraser, and one of his 'discoveries', Raymond Francis, veteran actress, Hazel Bainbridge, and Board chairman, Tony MacMillan, cut the anniversary cake exactly sixty years after the opening of the New Connaught Theatre

workshops were popular and the outreach department was expanding its activities. The only area in which there had been no development was the setting up of the resident production company: that idea had been allowed to creep away and die, as had the six-week closure in April and May.

Apart from Christmas and the summer musical there were usually ten or eleven mainstream touring shows for adults and two or three for children. A little ballet, opera, small scale drama and amateur shows made up the bulk of live entertainment.

The 1989/1990 season opened with high hopes.

CHAPTER THIRTEEN

The spring season of 1989 started well. Two performances of *La Traviata* by Welsh National Opera's small-scale tour department played to, remarkably, 104% capacity and made £412 (theatres hold 'house' seats back for Royalty or emergencies which enable them actually to sell more than the 100% of alleged capacity). Films did well, plays broke even, only dance and children's shows produced losses.

A notable contribution to the programme was a community project, the staging for six nights of Leonard Bernstein's *Mass* with orchestra, singers and dancers which, despite an audience of 78%, lost almost £7,000. A summer farce, *Bedside Manners*, with the immensely popular John Inman, lost almost £6,000 despite being seen by 2,000 people.

By the time of the summer show the year's losses stood at £2,579. Forty performances of *Underneath the Arches* with Bernie Winters pushed that figure up to over £6,000. Twenty-four showings of films managed to reduce the loss to £4,500 (despite one showing of *Empire of the Sun* attracting an audience of 8!)

The big success of the autumn was the Cambridge Theatre Company's production of Ayckbourn's *How the Other Half Loves* which brought in £3,144 (and almost lost Cambridge its Arts Council grant - subsidised companies were not expected to stage plays that audiences might actually want to see). This year's pantomime, *Snow White,* played to fewer than usual, only 81% of capacity, but nevertheless turned in £25,000; at the end of the year the total trading profit was just £25,500, half that of the previous twelve months.

There was a change of Administrator early in 1990, when David Popple, a former accountant comparatively new to the world of theatre, took over from Martin Harris who had moved on to the Chichester Festival Theatre. Harris had, of course, booked most of the opening shows for the year which, after two months, had turned in a loss of £10,000.

Plays joined dance in producing enormous losses: *The Entertainer* with Ben Warris, *Uncle Vanya* and Cheek by Jowl's *Sara* each lost over £3,300 and played to audiences varying between 55% and 34%. Even *Blues in the Night* with Stephanie Lawrence, which played to 76%, lost over £1,000.

Luckily seven showings of the film *Shirley Valentine* made over £3,500 - half of which was wiped out by the stage production of *Daisy Pulls it Off.*

The Spider's Web with Barbara Murray played to 2,875 (70%) and lost £6,000. Mollie Sugden in *Seaside Romp* lost another £3,300. However, films saved the day again and at the end of four months the losses were back down to £6,800.

The summer show, with Annabel Croft trying to sing in *Something's Afoot,* was truly awful and audiences were small but it was cheap (it showed) and actually made a profit of £4,100.

The autumn season got off to a dreadful start with *Tomfoolery*, playing to 1,741 and losing over £5,000. The only successful play came just before the pantomime; *The Woman in Black* was still playing at London's Fortune

Theatre when it came to the Connaught. Basically a two-hander, it was seen by 3,261 and made over £7,000.

For a change, when the pantomime - this time presented by Kevin Wood - opened there was an operating profit of almost £6,000 in hand.

Cinderella made a further £27,700 and despite losses totalling £3,500 by Diversions Dance Co. and English National Ballet, and a further £4,500 on Welsh National Opera's *Hansel and Gretel,* the end of year balance was £43,917 in credit.

Yet again, matters were about to change. 1991 was a bad year, the worst since the theatre reopened in 1986; the recession was in full swing, audiences plummeted and with them the trading profit.

The mayoral year was coming to a close in May and it was the centenary of Worthing being granted Borough status. It was suggested that, to round off the celebrations, the Connaught should work with the Brighton Actors Group to stage *The Importance of Being Earnest,* the comedy which Wilde had written whilst staying in the town almost a hundred years earlier.

The Brighton Actors' Group was a gathering of professional actors resident in the area who staged productions, usually in the Nightingale pub, when 'resting' - in other words, most of the time. The Connaught financed the production at £7,700, the 'sets', for want of a better word, were hired from Theatr Clwyd who had recently toured the play.

To suggest that the end result, done in the original - and rarely played - four-act version, was dreadful is possibly to over-praise it. It was doubly unfortunate that the previous week the Oxford Stage Company's excellent production of *The Seagull* had occupied the Connaught - comparisons were inevitable.

The Importance had a gala performance in the presence of the Mayor and Corporation on the Saturday night and helped to push up the week's audience to 1,139, though it did nothing for the theatre's reputation with the council. Nor did it alleviate a loss on the production of £5,800.

Was this the start of the rot? It may have been.

Unlike Martin Harris, who was always on show, David Popple emulated the Duke of Plaza Toro - he led his regiment from behind. A relaxed and laid-back character, he was rarely seen at first nights and few Worthing theatregoers knew him. His aim, though, was for quality; he wanted the highest standard available for Worthing and he would travel miles to find it. Unfortunately, quality in the world of theatre does not come cheap and the Connaught, with its capacity of only 514 seats and a top price of around £9, cannot compete with the neighbouring Brighton Theatre Royal, whose seating capacity is almost double and prices much higher. The problem is compounded when, in autumn and winter, the 1,375 seat Chichester Festival Theatre, just twenty miles away, also takes in touring shows. Guildford's Yvonne Arnaud Theatre, with a capacity of 590 (just 76 more than the Connaught), could afford expensive shows only by charging, then, up to £17 for seats, a figure Worthing residents would not dream of paying locally - though they might do elsewhere.

If Worthing was to have a good drama programme it seemed it was virtually forced to book companies which the town did not respond to, no matter how good they were. Cheek by Jowl's magnificent production of *As You Like It* drew an audience of only 1,324 (loss £2,376). Oxford Stage

Company's equally fine staging of Arthur Miller's *The Price* with Lynn Farleigh, Pip Donaghy and David Gant did slightly better at 1,672 (loss £1,273). Cambridge Theatre Company - less reliable in standard than the other two - lost £1,000 with Wycherley's *The Country Wife,* though it managed to make £700 with a totally lacklustre production of *Lady Windermere's Fan.*

What of commercial managements? If their product was good enough they wanted to go to Brighton and Chichester: if they came to Worthing the guarantee required was high and the risk became greater. Michael Rose Productions put in *The Great Gatsby,* a sizeable production with a large cast: it cost over £17,500 and took under £10,000.

Beyond Reasonable Doubt, however, similarly priced, did show a profit of £150 - Sir Jeffrey Archer's name pulled in 84% houses. Even a two-hander such as *Sleuth,* with Gerald Harper and Tony Anholt, cost £11,500 and lost £3,000 despite playing to 56% capacity.

Regency Opera did three performances of a passable *Tosca* with a large orchestra, no chorus and minimal sets at a cost of £9,000; playing to 70%, the loss was £290.

Worthing thinks it is a musical town - it was then (1991) the only town in the country with a full time director of music - and it supports a professional symphony orchestra. Yet, when Popple booked the renowned Borodin String Quartet, direct from playing at the Bath Festival, the audience numbered just 244.

Was the recession biting or had Worthing again grown tired of the Connaught as it had ever since the council first rescued the theatre? The honeymoon with Chris Denys had lasted barely a year. Ted Craig and Nic Young's successes in the 1970s lasted longer but the heyday of the 1980s was a flash in the pan. Despite growth in and around the town, Gillam's final audience figure of 2,500 was rarely exceeded twenty-five years later.

By July 1991 the loss was heading towards £8,000.

After the disappointing standard of the previous year's summer musical it was decided to try something different this time. It was exactly sixty years since repertory had first played at the old Connaught Hall and a celebration was called for.

Paul Darrow ('Avon' from the BBC series, *Blake's Seven*) brought together a small company to stage, in repertoire, *Gaslight, Relatively Speaking* and *Dial 'M' for Murder.* The ham was thick, the standard low and the audience absent. Worthing still does not like repertoire and the loss on the six weeks was £16,450. Luckily, some film matinees during the season had made £3,000.

When the autumn season opened the accumulated loss was running at more than £20,000; this was, surprisingly, reduced by a particularly poor play which starred Peter Duncan who had made a great personal success as Buttons in the previous Christmas pantomime: *Party Piece* was cheap to buy in and with an audience of under 1,800 it made a profit of £2,400: but quality it was not.

Kevin Wood put in *Babes in the Wood* at Christmas but it was poor. He was also staging *Mother Goose* at Brighton with John Inman and it was not difficult to see which was the better production. The Connaught's show suffered, too, from a dire script but if the Chairman of the Board wanted to write a panto who could stop him? However, audiences held up and the show more than covered the accumulated loss.

The winter season started well. Bill Kenwright was about to launch a new tour of the highly successful show, *Stepping Out.* Popple struck a deal which enabled the tour to open in Worthing and in return for dress-rehearsing on Monday and opening to the public on Tuesday the cost of the show was brought down to under £17,000. It played to 91% capacity and brought in nearly £20,000.

The year ended over £16,000 up - poor by previous standards but much better than had appeared likely at the start.

April 1992 saw the start of a run of disasters on the stage. The Cambridge Theatre Company's production of *The Revenger's Tragedy*, set in 1940s Hollywood, drove 25% or more of the audience out at or before the interval on most nights. These were mainly the more mature playgoers: when the company returned in the autumn with a starkly peculiar production of the rarely seen *Lulu* it was the younger generation that walked out.

(What theatre companies do not seem to realise is that theatregoers of any age who do not sit through an entire performance leave the theatre angry, angry at the waste of time and the waste of money. They do not forgive quickly and they stay away. Sometimes they stay away for three or four productions, sometimes they stay away for three or four months or even years.)

But it was not only subsidised theatre that caused walk-outs that year. A dreadful play based on Jerome K. Jerome's backstage experiences, *Stagelands,* should never have reached the stage at all.

Few, if any, walked out of *See How They Run*, but it was dated and past its 'sell-by date', although well acted by Josephine Tewson and Jon Iles. By the time it reached Worthing a long tour of *Witness for the Prosecution* was tired and dusty. The alleged British premiere of Feydeau's farce, *Pig in a Poke,* proved he could write dire stuff as well as comic masterpieces. One could only wonder what on earth persuaded Channel Theatre Company that *The Haunted Hotel* was either thrilling or entertaining.

Why did you book them, people asked. Didn't you see them first? Unfortunately, these days the programme is booked months in advance, long before a production goes into rehearsal or is even being cast.

But as had happened before, that year's drama was more evident off stage than on.

With the 1967 extension of the stage way out into the auditorium, in front of the proscenium arch, the safety curtain was suspended half way back. Whilst the theatre was building its own sets they could be constructed so as to allow the safety curtain to be lowered. With touring shows, however, this was rarely possible, and the Fire Brigade frequently had to be asked to suspend their regulations that the safety curtain must be lowered in the presence of every audience. This was usually granted - they simply increased the number of appliances that they would send to the theatre in the event of an emergency. It now seemed that this was becoming a permanent feature and the Fire Safety Officer decided the time had come to insist on the installation of a new safety curtain.

The council agreed to install a new roller-style curtain to cut off the auditorium completely from the stage area in the event of fire. This would entail considerable installation work, taking about two months during which the stage could not be used for productions. It was decided that the best time to do this would be in the summer and so, instead of a show, films were planned for July and August.

As work began, the costs seemed to escalate daily. Luckily the football pools promoters, with government co-operation, had set up the Foundation for Sport and the Arts, not to replace the Arts Council grants, but to assist in ancillary activities.

Popple worked hard to formulate an acceptable application for funds from the Foundation and successfully prevented the costs falling on the town's poll-tax payers.

At about the same time the Arts Council was holding one of its competitions designed to waste the time of already overworked theatre staff. Applications were invited for a share in an 'audience development' fund. Popple, with his marketing assistant, Jakki Hall, spent hours filling in forms and creating hypothetical situations which could have resulted in failure. Fortunately they were rewarded with £5,000 in the current (1992/93) financial year and £15,000 for the following year.

Meanwhile matters were stirring at the Borough Council. A report had just been received from the independent accountants Price Waterhouse which examined value for money in the provision of civic sponsored culture and entertainment in the town. The MACE report, as it was called, had been insisted upon for all local authorities by central government. When the report on Worthing arrived it was thrown out by the Entertainments and Tourism Committee as being out of date and too inaccurate to be of any service. Another report, however, was looked at with far more interest. This had been compiled by Hywel Griffiths, the town's Entertainments and Tourism chief. He too had looked at all aspects of the local entertainment scene and one of his chapters concerned the Connaught.

Though acknowledging that the Connaught fulfilled a need and was well run, Griffiths concluded that it would be more economically managed, not as a separate entity, but as part of the Entertainments and Tourism department.

The chairman of Worthing's Policy and Resources Committee of the Council, responsible for the town's budget, was Cllr Eric Macdonald who had always been opposed to the Connaught's grant. The town had to save over £420,000 in its 1993/94 expenditure to avoid government charge-capping, and the Committee decided that at least 25% of this should come from the arts and entertainment provision - then running at over £1 million.

At a meeting of Connaught management and Board representatives with members of the budget sub-committee and council officers, the proposal to make the savings by taking the theatre back into council control was put forward. (Nobody, it seems, mentioned that on the two previous occasions when it had been in council control - 1966/67 and most of 1986 - it had been dark!)

The Connaught representatives queried the statistics which had been produced to support the proposal, which they thought were unreliable. They also turned the argument on its head by asking if 'independence' for the pier and the Assembly Hall had been considered - it had not.

The most recent figures available (for the year ending 31 March, 1992) showed that attendances at the Connaught had been 93,542, against only 90,518 for both the pier and the Assembly Hall. The subsidy per seat at the Connaught with its 514 capacity had been £4.10 while the pier (870 seats) had cost the council £7.55 and the Assembly Hall (926 seats) £10.46. The Connaught, too, could quantify its marketing costs at £77,295 while the expenditure of the other two venues was included in the council's overall advertising and publicity budget of £263,915. Given these figures, council representatives had to accept that they should give the Connaught an opportunity to submit revised proposals.

The meeting had taken place on the evening of Monday, 18 January; the Connaught's figures had to be ready for final discussion that Thursday.

By slightly reducing its programme and by agreeing to transfer its marketing activities to the council, the Connaught considered it could work with a grant of £120,000. The council was happy to accept the revised proposition.

But how would such a drastic cut affect the theatre? The press was told 'the Board has every confidence in the future of the theatre.'

In the past any such threat to the Connaught would have been met with howls of outrage, demonstrations and petitions. This time there was hardly a murmur. Perhaps Worthing really had lost interest in its theatre.

Economies had to be made. Popple was not universally popular with the Board. He was not there on first nights, he would not book cheaper shows and he had contracted Welsh National Opera Company's production of *Macbeth* for three nights instead of the usual two (because its visit coincided with the Brighton festival); these factors all acted against him. Staff morale was low and had been for some time: this also was blamed on him (only partially correct, all three members of the management team were at fault here). But above all, reserves had been sacrificed, though whether that was the fault of the administration, the recession or Worthing's tastes it was difficult to tell.

The axes were being sharpened again and they were being wielded by the same people who had done the deed in 1985.

Popple was summoned to appear with, if he wished, a 'friend', before a sub-committee of the Board - at which, surprisingly, since the Board was an 'independent' organisation, the council's personnel officer was present. A subsequent press release announced: 'David Popple, the Theatre Administrator of the Connaught, whose last three years in office have vastly increased the profile and reputation of the venue, feels that the financial constraints under which the theatre will have to operate in the next financial year: with the grant having being (sic) effectively halved and the marketing activities now being joined with that of the Borough's Theatre section, will not allow him to continue as he would have wished and, accordingly, he has asked to be released from his contract.

'Therefore, he and the Board after a prolonged discussion have decided to part company.

'The Board regrets the circumstances which have brought this about and wishes David the best of luck in the future.

'The theatre will now be jointly managed by Stephen Holroyd and David Smith, the Theatre Manager and Administration Manager respectively, in whom the Board have every confidence.'

No mention was made of the slightly over £15,000 compensation the Board paid to Popple, since his contract did not expire for another twelve months. Coincidentally this sum was almost equal to the Arts Council Audience Development grant for 1993/94 which he had won.

Popple soon found himself another administrative post within the arts world and two of the productions which he had booked into the Connaught for April, *Sweet Revenge* with Richard Todd, and the English Shakespeare Company's *Romeo and Juliet* were both very successful. Visits by the Welsh National Opera, English

National Ballet and the Cambridge Theatre Company's *Long Day's Journey into Night,* however, were not.

Stephen Holroyd had been in the world of theatre for over twenty-five years and was a highly respected technician; David Smith, like Popple, was a trained accountant. The economies soon began to show: marketing had all but gone, 'outreach' virtually so, Saturday jazz in the bar ended and even the bar itself was no longer open all day. Staff discontent grew worse. To replace the jazz a self-indulgent 'radio serial' was presented in the bar each Saturday morning by an amalgam of Board members and local amateur actors - the much-vaunted professionalism had gone too.

But on stage it was a good autumn. *An Evening with Gary Lineker,* presented by the Colchester Mercury Theatre, brought in a young, eager and vibrant audience many of whom came back again a couple of weeks later for *Hamlet.* This was the first production by English Touring Theatre, a company born out of a rather tatty touring group called Century Theatre: a new director had taken over, determined to take good productions of classics and new plays to the regions. Alan Cumming and Eleanor Bron led an excellent company in *Hamlet* and subsequent productions the company has brought to the Connaught have continued, almost without exception, to be of an equally high standard.

The biggest attraction of that autumn came to Worthing by chance. Michael Rose was touring *The Cemetery Club,* starring Anne Charleson, Millicent Martin and Judy Cornwell. It had played both Brighton and Chichester but Rose suddenly found himself with a vacant week in October and offered it to Worthing. Unless the Connaught could take it, the production would have to go 'off the road' for the week which would prove very expensive and so an affordable deal was offered.

The production was stylish and polished. Box office records were broken, proving that Worthing still had an audience for quality productions with 'star' names. Unfortunately after this both seemed suddenly to disappear.

As the Connaught headed towards its sixtieth anniversary caution was the watchword. Many of the shows appeared to be cheap, with spartan settings, small casts and, sometimes, very bad acting. During the interval of the first presentation of 1994, *Tom Jones, the Musical,* the few members of the audience who decided to stay on for the second act were vying with each other to recall anything worse they had ever seen - within twelve months they were destined to see several more productions which were, incredibly, very much worse. *Sleeping it Off* (another dire Feydeau piece), *Wait Until Dark* and *Dangerous Corner* (not the acclaimed Chichester Festival Theatre's production which had just closed) showed British theatre at its worst.

Fortunately English Touring Theatre was back with two classics, *A Doll's House* and *As You Like It,* which reminded audiences how inspiring good theatre can be. A year later they made amends for the Brighton Actors Group by bringing to the Connaught a wonderfully inventive, but faithful to the script, production of *The Importance of Being Earnest.* The haughty Lady Bracknell was superbly played by the drag queen Bette Bourne.

The nadir, however, was reached with a touring production of *Murder at the Vicarage,* with another drag queen George Logan (better known as the Dr Evadne Hinge half of Hinge & Bracket) as Miss Marple. The set wobbled, shoes and hair styles were quite out of period, the actors had no idea of characterisation, the direction was non-existent and the press notices were appalling. Fraser, Verney and Gillam must have turned in their graves. Productions like these would never have reached the stage in their days - weekly rep may be decried by those who never saw it but in Worthing it never sank as low as this.

With Christmas, however, spirits soared: *Cinderella,* staged by Muffin Productions, was a magical pantomime, a joy for all age groups. A year that, overall, had been poor for quality but reasonable for finances ended on a high note.

1995 opened to complete chaos! David Smith, who booked all the shows and films was ill. Muffin Productions, who were contracted to stage the next pantomime, *Jack and the Beanstalk* - for which tickets were already being sold - had gone bust. There were problems galore in the bar: it had been decided to hand the catering over to a private contractor who, days before he was due to take over, pulled out. The opening hours were cut drastically, it was alleged that there were stock deficiencies and both the bar manager and the catering supervisor were sacked.

Staff morale was at its lowest, with virtually everyone looking for new jobs but still working like slaves. The marketing department suddenly found itself in charge of the box office and the young, underpaid staff were working seventy hours or more a week without any hope of overtime pay. A return visit by *The Lion, the Witch and the Wardrobe* did not repeat its original success and some performances had to be aborted. A well publicised illustrated talk by John Huntley on *'Picture Palaces and their Organs'* had to be cancelled at the last moment when it was discovered that no contracts had ever been signed and he was engaged elsewhere on the night in question.

The standard of shows was nevertheless higher than in the previous year, though a 'big name' production of *Brideshead Revisited* was a disappointment. Films were now bringing in big audiences throughout the country with *Four Weddings and a Funeral* proving particularly popular in its several screenings at the Connaught.

And so the Connaught began to think of celebrating its sixty years as a theatre.

Since the reopening in 1986 it had saluted its roots on several occasions. Bill Fraser had died in 1987, a year after winning an Olivier Award for comedy performance of the year as the drunken photographer in a revival of Priestley's *When We Are Married* at the Whitehall Theatre (the cast also included Patricia Routledge and Elizabeth Spriggs). On 20 March 1989, his widow, Pamela Cundell, unveiled a plaque in the foyer commemorating his pioneering work at the Connaught, and a couple of years later the theatre bar was revamped and is now known as Fraser's Bar.

In April, 1994, Mark Wynter unveiled a tribute to Melville Gillam and four months after that, in an evening entitled *From Worthing to Westminster,* Glenda Jackson, MP, told a packed house of her experiences since making her professional stage debut at the Connaught in 1957.

It was obvious that the theatre did not have the funds for a big splash to mark the sixtieth anniversary on 30 September, but as it happened two of Gillam's protégés were on stage that day. A revival of *Doctor in the House* had been playing a summer season on the pier at Bournemouth and its management, E & B Productions, sent it on an autumn tour with a company which included Ted Rogers, whose panto debut had been as Buttons in the 1956 Connaught *Cinderella,* and Peggy Sinclair, a very popular leading lady of the Worthing Theatre Company at the same period.

It was arranged that they would jointly host a party held in the bar after the matinee on the Saturday. That the party was after the matinee and not the evening performance meant the celebrations were rather sober but actors on tour, understandably, want to travel home as soon as possible after the week's final performance.

Doctor in the House had been staged twice in the days of weekly rep and since Peggy Sinclair had been in the 1957 production and her husband, Richard Coleman, had played Sir Launcelot six years later, it was decided to invite as many as could be found of the cast of those two productions to a tea and wine party.

Not all members of the two companies could be traced, and many of those who could were working. Glenda Jackson, Daniel Massey, Elizabeth Spriggs, Roland Curram and Peter Byrne (who, incidentally, had been the original 'B' of E & B Productions) sent their apologies, but there was a packed matinee audience to welcome Ann Castle and her husband, Alan Bridges (who had directed the first production), Hazel Bainbridge and her daughter, Belinda Carroll, Richard Coleman and Amanda Walker together with many of the original technicians who still lived in the town.

This production of *Doctor in the House* bore little resemblance to its previous showings in Worthing - it was designed for a summer holiday audience that wanted plenty of ad-libbing and very little acting from the TV comedians who headed the cast and this was not what the elderly Worthing matinee audience had expected. They looked at the familiar faces of those actors sitting among them, they remembered the sparkling performances they had seen Peggy Sinclair give and those greying and white-haired heads shook: it never used to be like this.

CHAPTER FOURTEEN

When cinema audiences decided to stay at home and watch television or videos the film makers hit back. Instead of concentrating on trash for teenagers they started to make films that the public would want to see - films of all types catering for all tastes and all ages from young children to their great grandparents.

As an accountant David Smith knew that if the Connaught was to keep within its budget, films had to be a major part of his programming. He knew that the Borough Council's grant was going down each year while expenses were going up. Although his regular playgoers might moan about the standard of the plays and companies he had booked, he knew, too, that financially it was preferable to have cheap shows than quality productions which lost money. Of the three administrators running the Connaught since 1986 he alone could boast that money had not been lost on the drama seasons - though Oxford Stage Company's critically acclaimed *Roots* had threatened to rock the boat very severely.

In 1995, with the National Lottery having millions of pounds to spend on supporting the Arts, the Connaught's Board decided to re-open the Ritz as a studio theatre/cinema to seat 275. The old theatre was to be tidied up at a cost of about £40,000, benefactors were asked to contribute £50 each to buy new seating and it was planned to launch a public appeal for funds to restore the venue to its former glory with substantial help from the Lottery.

Unfortunately the venture got off to an inauspicious start: audiences complained that the seats were uncomfortable (they were), that the sound was bad (it was) and that the building looked derelict (it did). There was some understanding when it was explained that the Ritz was in its early stages of restoration but although a lot of work was carried out it did not become a popular venue with cinemagoers. When a film was given some screenings in the main house and some in the Ritz most patrons chose to go to the main house.

Volunteers worked hard on formulating a Lottery bid, but to succeed the Connaught Board needed both partnership funding (Lottery money would fund only a proportion of any restoration or development project) and a lease from the Borough Council. Neither was forthcoming and the idea was dropped.

Meanwhile the council, which ran Worthing Symphony Orchestra, had been advised by an independent consultant that its control and management should be in the hands of a separate trust. What a bit of luck that the Connaught had not been taken back into the council's domain in 1993 - here was a readymade trust still fairly firmly in the municipality's grip which could now take over the band.

Suddenly the Board was running a theatre, a cinema and an orchestra!

Despite the planned opening of large new venues in Salford, Milton Keynes and other towns, the run up to the new millennium has not been an easy time for theatres anywhere. Chichester Festival Theatre had to plead for public funding to keep its doors open. Others, like Cheltenham and Bolton, found that with the Arts Council and Regional Arts Boards cutting or removing subsidies they either had to follow the Connaught and rely entirely on touring shows or use them to supplement a reduction in home produced work. But this, it seemed, had a beneficial effect on the touring circuit, for at the start of 1999 the number and quality of productions taking to the road suddenly increased.

With the relocating and enlargement of Sir Alan Ayckbourn's Stephen Joseph Theatre in Scarborough, he had for the first time a small auditorium with an end-on stage. When he decided to take his *Haunting Julia* on a winter tour to nine of the smaller venues round the country he asked the Connaught if it would be interested in having it. The result was one of the most outstanding productions that Worthing had seen in the past five years, with a particularly fine setting and excellent acting. And *Haunting Julia* had followed a particularly successful pantomime.

Like Gillam many years earlier, the theatre had decided to stop 'buying in' its Christmas production, and started to organise, cast and present its own. The first two shows seemed somewhat tentative but the 1998/99 production of *Aladdin* with Mark Little and Linda Nolan was absolutely brimming with confidence and panache.

The theatre was brimming with confidence, too, in its new subscription scheme. 'See four shows for only £20' was the offer, a saving of £20 on the top ticket price. The programme was attractive, to follow the Ayckbourn play were productions of Tom Stoppard's *On the Razzle*, some well-known faces in Agatha Christie's *And Then There Were None* and finally the West End hit comedy, *Women on the Verge of HRT.* The deal attracted 572 new purchasers and brought back 170 who had let previous subscriptions lapse. The total take-up amounted to 1,424, more than double subscription holders in the previous season and equivalent to almost three full houses in a seven performance run. After such an auspicious opening to the season it looked as though the Connaught was riding high.

That winter season was good for films, too, with such hits as *Little Voice* and *Shakespeare in Love* doing brisk business.

Yet again everything, it seemed, was coming up roses and yet again disaster loomed.

The future of the Dome cinema, which the council had owned for some time, was causing problems. The eighty-nine year old building was in a dilapidated state, still using projection equipment from the 1930s, still with mono sound and it had been made a Listed building. Although the ornate dome had been refurbished the council was reluctant to spend any more on it.

The building was put up for sale but the only offer which seemed to have any viability was £10 from a body of local enthusiasts who had formed the Dome Preservation Trust. Their plan, if successful, was to apply for Lottery funding to reinstate the elaborate interior and run it as a two-screen cinema, with a film museum and tourist information office.

For some while the Dome had been operated by Robins Cinemas on a succession of short-term leases from the council. Despite the Connaught, too, showing films the growing number of cinema buffs in the town, many of them of the younger generation, complained that many of the latest releases were not coming to Worthing and they had to travel to Brighton, Chichester or Bognor Regis to see them.

Then, just as the Connaught's fortunes seemed to be changing, outline planning permission was given for a new nine-screen multiplex at Teville Gate, a stone's throw from the theatre. Although final plans had still to be submitted to the council, it was generally expected that the new venture would open sometime in the year 2001. If this was not a big enough problem for the Connaught to face an even bigger spanner was suddenly thrown in the works. In the middle of March the council announced that an inspection of the Dome had revealed it was in a dangerous condition, too dangerous to allow it to remain open for public use. The current lease to Robins Cinemas was due to expire on 5 April when the Dome would close.

Just days after it had been boarded up (at, presumably, no little cost to council taxpayers) a further engineer's survey showed that the situation was nowhere near as bad as had been thought and repairs could possibly have been completed within a week. But it was too late: the Dome was closed, fourteen people had lost their jobs and there would probably be no full-time cinema in Worthing for another two years.

On Tuesday, 20 April 1999, all twelve full-time staff, the 30 part-timers and the volunteers who helped in the running of the Connaught were called to a meeting with the Chairman and the Administrator. They were told that David Smith had found it impossible to produce a budget for the coming year and that at an emergency Board meeting the previous evening it had been agreed that the management and running of the Connaught should become the direct responsibility of the Borough Council from July.

There would be a pool of employees, front of house and back stage, to operate all the town's venues and inevitably many of the Connaught staff could expect to lose their jobs. The Ritz was to become a full-time cinema, the auditorium being completely refurbished, reseated and carpeted at a cost estimated to be in the region of £50,000.

Drama, they were told, would remain the core of the Connaught's programming, but instead of staging an average of twelve full weeks of live productions each year as well as many one-night shows, there would in future be just six plays staged between September and March (a pip rather than a core, perhaps?). The Worthing Musical Comedy Society would continue to stage its shows at the Connaught which, for the next two years at least, would also have a pantomime. All other productions, such as opera, ballet, children's shows and one-nighters, would now go to the Pavilion. Apart from around 12 weeks of the year the Connaught would go back to its original function as a cinema.

A couple of days later the Chief Executive's Department of the Borough Council issued a press release headlined 'Cinema to Continue in Worthing'.

'The Council and the Board [of the Connaught Theatre] have been discussing a package of proposals which maintains the capacity for popular films to be shown in the town, protects the Connaught's role as a venue for live drama, and adds a new dimension to arts development in the town through the appointment by the Council of an 'Arts Development Manager'. If the Dome reopens in the short term, the council has pledged to co-operate with the Trust, or operator, to ensure complementary programming. The Board agreed on Monday to offer proposals which will now be put to the Council's Committees.

'The Board have agreed to council proposals that this new setup will best be run by the council. The Theatre Board has, therefore, agreed to relinquish control of the Connaught to the council. In due course the Charitable Company operating the theatre will be wound up. Tony MacMillan was then said to have stated 'Although we are sad to see the end of the Company's role in the Theatre, we can all look back on the past thirteen years as a period of great success in giving the town what it has obviously wanted, including the development of the Ritz as a flexible multi-purpose venue in the centre of town. Now the prospect is something entirely different. The important issue is the future of the artistic activities, not any one building, company or person.'

It all sounded very amicable and agreeable but that is not how one Board member, Mel Denman saw it: 'All the Board bar one was present, together with the Treasurer and Secretary, both Borough Council officers. We were presented with a document which had been produced by the Borough Council and David Smith and were told there was nothing the Board could do about this. We voted in principle for all entertainment to come under one umbrella. We had to, it was a fait accompli. I said it would be a heyday for the Council for a couple of years, with films making such a good profit, but that to cut down drama was short-sighted. What was the plan for when the multiplex is open and the Connaught and Ritz have no audience?, I asked. One Board member, a councillor, started quoting from what we assumed was the same report: but it appears he had another referring to the lease of the car park next door to the Connaught coming up for renewal in a year's time and the probability that the police station [the only other building on the same side of Union Place as the Connaught] would be relocating within two years.

'When I was invited to join the Connaught Board two years ago, I wrote in my acceptance to Tony MacMillan that my prime consideration was for the Connaught, its staff and its continuation as a theatre. I now had no option but to resign.'

Tony MacMillan, too, resigned at the next Board meeting. 'It has been suggested that the Board has been an integral part of the negotiations which is patently untrue,' he said. 'In a press release my original quote was written for me by an officer who made no contact at all.'

Although the press release stated that the new Arts Development Manager would come from the existing Connaught staff, it failed to name David Smith who had already accepted the post.

The timing of the meetings and these announcements was not propitious. The Liberal Democrat-controlled council was in recess pending the local elections. The idea that there was a 'hidden agenda' to allow the Connaught to become part of a redevelopment scheme rapidly gained credence, especially when a Conservative councillor confirmed it was a possibility.

In fact control of the council changed at the election and within a few days the new Conservative administration announced that it had moved to make the Connaught a listed building so that there could be no possibility of redevelopment.

Two items were on the agenda of a special meeting of the Policy and Resources Committee which came a few days later: the future of both the Dome and of the Connaught. Although English Heritage said it would not be able to give its decision on Lottery funding for the cinema until September instead of July as originally expected, it seemed quite feasible to reopen the theatre within a matter of weeks. Certainly it was the wish of both parties that this should happen as quickly as possible.

Both parties, too, were insistent that when the Dome reopened the pressure to use the Connaught for films would be greatly reduced and that it should return to the presentation of high quality stage shows.

Councillor Jonathan Howcroft-Stemp, the new Chairman of the Leisure Services Committee, declared 'I want to see a multiplex in the town but I want, too, a live theatre.'

Worthing spends a lot of money on arts and entertainment. It has a good museum and art gallery, the orchestra, the Assembly Hall, the Pavilion and a smaller venue at Field Place often used for amateur drama.

Although the Pavilion is a typical 1920s multi-purpose seaside venue, it is well run, staging possibly the most extensive programme of entertainment anywhere on the south coast with something for everyone. Worthing is too small to attract the international mega-stars who visit the Brighton Centre, but in recent years people of the calibre of Victor Borge, Lesley Garrett, Howard Keel, top comedians and 'name' groups popular with youngsters have all appeared in the town. Recently, catering for the public's demand for musicals, the Pavilion, despite its limited stage facilities, has presented Paul Nicholas in *The Pirates of Penzance,* Peter Duncan in *Barnum*, the Russian Ice Stars and Bill Kenright's *Joseph and the Amazing Technicolor Dreamcoat.*

But where does the Connaught fit in?

Back in 1986, when Patrick Boyd Maunsell prepared his report on the way ahead, he went against current thinking by proposing seasons of plays by a resident company. The likelihood is that such a company would in fact win more loyal support than touring shows, but since the reopening of the Ritz the Connaught no longer has workshop space so a return to 'in-house' productions, even for 18 weeks a year, would be difficult.

Boyd Maunsell also identified the need to let out the theatre to amateur groups at a subsidised rental for around six weeks a year. The Ritz has been used for some amateur drama but the only company using the main house now is the Worthing Musical Comedy Society - all the town's other groups use the Pavilion.

Over the past twelve years there have been two very big community projects at the Connaught. Eight years after the 1989 presentation of Leonard Bernstein's *Mass*, *Rough Music! Rough Justice!,* a huge musical based on episodes in the town's history was staged with a cast of over 100. Enterprises of this nature are, however, by virtue of their cost, few and far between.

In 1931 Gwladys Wheeler thought Worthing a town of intellectual snobs: is that still so today? Certainly the past few years have shown that unless there are well-known names in the cast, Worthing audiences for a play can be small, no matter how good the production.

There is, however, a strong nucleus of theatre-lovers in the area: 'Theatrecard', a scheme set up by David Popple for Connaught supporters, has a mailing list of 580. In the Borough itself, never mind the surrounding areas, 353 residents support the Chichester Festival Theatre Society and the local branch of the Theatregoers Club of Great Britain has around 250 members enjoying coach trips to theatres all over the south east.If the Connaught is to succeed as a theatre there has to be two-way action: the council needs to discover what it is that people will go to see and the public must realise it is only bums on seats, not signatures on petitions, that will keep the place open.

With the number of films now being shown it seems as though the wheel has turned almost full circle. The great danger is that when the films stop the council will, as it did in 1930, declare that it is no longer prepared to support live drama in the town. Just listing the building may not be enough to save it.

But whatever the Connaught's future it can be proud of the influential part it has played in British theatre history.

Index